COLORED
GEMSTONES

Books by Antoinette Matlins

(all GemStone Press)

DIAMONDS: THE ANTOINETTE MATLINS BUYING GUIDE
*How to Select, Buy, Care for & Enjoy Diamonds
with Confidence and Knowledge*

THE PEARL BOOK: THE DEFINITIVE BUYING GUIDE
How to Select, Buy, Care for & Enjoy Pearls
2nd edition

JEWELRY & GEMS: THE BUYING GUIDE
*How to Buy Diamonds, Pearls, Colored Gemstones, Gold & Jewelry
with Confidence and Knowledge*

GEM IDENTIFICATION MADE EASY
A Hands-On Guide to More Confident Buying & Selling
2nd edition

ENGAGEMENT & WEDDING RINGS
The Definitive Buying Guide for People in Love
2nd edition

COLORED GEMSTONES

The Antoinette Matlins Buying Guide

How to Select, Buy, Care for & Enjoy
Sapphires, Emeralds, Rubies
and Other Colored Gems
with Confidence and Knowledge

Antoinette Matlins, P.G.

GEMSTONE PRESS
Woodstock, Vermont

Colored Gemstones
The Antoinette Matlins Buying Guide

Library of Congress Cataloging-in-Publication Data

Matlins, Antoinette Leonard.
Colored gemstones—the Antoinette Matlins buying guide : how to select, buy, care for & enjoy sapphires, emeralds, rubies and other colored gems with confidence and knowledge / Antoinette L. Matlins.
          p. cm.
Includes bibliographical references and index.
ISBN 0-943763-33-9
1. Gems. I. Title. II. Title: Antoinette Matlins buying guide. III. Title: How to select, buy, care for & enjoy sapphires, emeralds, rubies and other colored gems with confidence and knowledge.
TS740.M38 2001
553.8'4—dc21

2001003722

10 9 8 7 6 5 4 3 2 1
Manufactured in Canada

Cover Design: Stacey Hood
Interior Design: Chelsea Cloeter
Color Insert: Bridgett Taylor

GemStone Press
A Division of LongHill Partners, Inc.
Sunset Farm Offices, Route 4, P.O. Box 237
Woodstock, VT 05091
Tel: (802) 457-4000   Fax: (802) 457-4004
www.gemstonepress.com

Contents

PART ONE Getting to Know Gems

PART TWO Colored Gemstones

PART THREE
Important Advice Before & After You Buy

Appendix

Index 178

Price Guides

Special Charts and Tables

Color Photograph Section

Acknowledgments

There are many people who have helped me learn and understand the complexities of this exciting field—too many to try to mention all of them here. Nonetheless, there are a few people who have been especially influential and supportive of the work I have done, and I would like to take a moment to acknowledge them. In addition to my father, I would like to thank my brother Kenneth Bonanno, F.G.A., P.G., and my sisters Karen Bonanno DeHaas, F.G.A., P.G., and Kathryn Bonanno Patrizzi, F.G.A., P.G., from whom I continue to learn, and with whom I enjoy sharing and debating gemological issues. I would also like to thank, in particular, C.R. "Cap" Beesley, Director of American Gemological Laboratories, New York; he has been a great teacher, and his research and leadership have benefited the entire gem and jewelry community.

I would also like to thank Robert Crowningshield, former Vice President of the Gemological Institute of America (GIA). A wonderful friend to my father, he has always been generous in the time he has given me to address questions or issues I might have. Mr. Crowningshield's work for the past half-century in the field of colored gemstones, and his contributions to the gemological literature, have helped shape the world of gemology as we know it.

At GemStone Press I would like to thank Sandra Korinchak, Polly Mahoney, and Bridgett Taylor, with whom it has been a pleasure to work, and who have made the project fun.

And last, but not least, I want to thank my husband, Stuart Matlins, for his unfailing support and encouragement, and for his willingness to spend many lonely nights while I'm traveling around the world to pursue my work.

Dedication

This book is specially dedicated to my father, Antonio C. Bonanno, who died in 1996. He inspired me as a child and filled my world with awe and wonder. He was my teacher, my mentor, and my coauthor on three books. Although his name is not on this cover, his knowledge and wisdom—his words, his ideas, his values—fill its pages. My gratitude is eternal.

Colored gemstones were my father's first love, and so I felt his presence keenly as I worked on this volume. As one of the first gemologists to fully disclose gemstone treatments to his clients, and as Founding Father of the Accredited Gemologists Association—through which he and other gemologists worldwide have strongly advocated for full disclosure for almost twenty-five years—his influence is clearly present in this volume. This book could not be what it is without his indelible mark.

Preface

Whatever gem or jewel you are seeking, with each passing year there are more choices than ever. There are recently discovered "new" gemstones, and gems in sensuous new colors; there are exciting new cutting styles that are creating greater brilliance and scintillation; and there are award-winning designers creating exquisite pieces in which to display them. For anyone who loves color and the world of gemstones, this is the most exciting time in history.

Having so many gemstone choices can be confusing, however, if you don't understand how one gem compares to another in terms of the unique characteristics of each and differences in wearability, rarity, and cost. More importantly, there are many more things to look *out* for, and more reasons *not* to base your choice on price alone. Now more than ever, understanding as much as possible about what you are buying is the key to getting what you really want, paying the right price, and enjoying your gem and jewelry purchases for years to come.

My first book, *Jewelry & Gems: The Buying Guide,* which I wrote with my father in the early 1980s, was the first book ever written to help consumers and lay people understand what they were really buying. It provided step-by-step guidance to make the purchase of diamonds, colored gemstones, pearls, and gold jewelry safer, less confusing, and more pleasurable. Now, almost twenty years, five editions, and over 250,000 copies later, in English, Arabic, Greek, Russian, and Spanish, the information it provides remains indispensable. But with each updated edition of *Jewelry & Gems,* it became increasingly difficult to cover all that was happening in the world of colored gemstones. As I began the fifth edition, it became clear that there was just too much additional information on colored gemstones to try to incorporate it into a single volume inclusive of diamonds, pearls, and gold as well. Thus *Colored Gemstones: The*

Antoinette Matlins Buying Guide was created. While some of the information here is also found in *Jewelry & Gems,* it has been edited to focus on colored gemstones, and it contains more extensive information about colored gemstones.

Today's colored gemstone market reflects the best of times and the worst of times: beautiful gemstones abound—in more colors, shapes, and designs than ever before—but today's jewelry counters are also filled with imitations, synthetics, and artificially enhanced gemstones. Where synthetics are concerned, almost *any* gem can now be created in a laboratory, and many are so good that they have been erroneously identified and sold as natural gems. And *most* colored gemstones are being routinely treated to look like the rarer, more beautiful gems of bygone eras (see chapters 5 and 6). As with all my other books, this book gives you all the information you really need in order to make wiser choices and reduce the risk especially inherent when buying or selling colored gemstones.

One area of special focus deals with enhancement techniques used to alter the appearance of colored gemstones. While we discussed gemstone treatments candidly in the first edition of *Jewelry & Gems: The Buying Guide* back in 1984, they have only recently become the focus of media stories and captured the public's attention. Today treatments are even more widespread, and are used for an increasing number of gemstones, so it is more important than ever before to understand the marketplace in order to be sure you get what you really want, and pay the right price for what you get. While covered in chapter 6, I would like to comment here on this situation.

Exceptionally fine *natural* gemstones are rarer and more costly than ever before. This scarcity has affected what is available in jewelry stores, and the choices available to consumers. *Natural* emeralds, rubies, and sapphires—that is, gems not subjected to any type of artificial treatment or enhancement—have never been rarer than they are today. While they can still be found, locating a natural gem in a particular size and quality can take months of intensive searching, and when one is found, it can command a price prohibitive to all but the most serious collector or connoisseur. I was recently retained to help a couple acquire an exceptionally fine Colombian emerald. After discussing the options with me, and learning about different fillers and degrees of treatment used on emerald, they were willing to accept a stone with "minor traces of oil." They did not want a stone treated with other types of filler, however, nor a stone with more than minimal treatment. It took many months to find the 3.64-carat emerald they selected, and the cost—at wholesale—was almost $100,000! Helping another couple search for an exceptionally fine 5-carat natural sapphire of Kashmir origin took almost as long, and the wholesale cost was over $50,000. This is not what most people usually want, and most retail jewelers don't keep such gems in their regular inventory.

As the beauty and overall quality of natural gemstones available in the marketplace began to decline over the past few decades, more and more enhanced gems were introduced in an effort to meet an ever-increasing demand for beautiful ruby, emerald, sapphire, and other gemstone jewelry. Given a choice, most people seeking a lovely piece of jewelry would rather have a treated gem, at an affordable price, than spend the time and money necessary to find a natural gem and obtain proper documentation of its authenticity. As a result, virtually *all* colored gemstones sold routinely in jewelry stores are treated, including the most important salons worldwide.

There is nothing wrong with buying an enhanced gem as long as you know the gem is enhanced, pay a fair price for it, and have been advised as to whether or not its appearance could change at some future time (see chapters 5 and 6). Anyone buying any colored gemstone sold in jewelry stores today should assume it has been treated in some way and should make sure it has been priced appropriately for what it is. Keep in mind that, unfortunately, many salespeople do not know about treatments and, as a result, fail to disclose this information. In some cases, salespeople really believe that the stones they sell are "natural" and sell them as such, even when this is not the case.

The extensive use of treatments has led to greater reliance on reports from respected gem-testing laboratories, and I encourage anyone buying a fine, rare, "natural" colored gemstone to make sure it has accompanying documentation from a respected laboratory. However, the presence of a laboratory report accompanying a gem is not a guarantee, and you must understand what should be included and how to read a colored gemstone report (see chapter 4). It is also important to know that the increased use of lab reports has resulted in an increase in reports from laboratories that are not reliable and fraudulent reports attributed to respected laboratories, so you must also be sure to verify the laboratory and the report attributed to it, and make sure the report relates to the gem you are buying.

For those who prefer only natural stones, some jewelers now offer sapphire, ruby, and emerald in a wider quality range to provide options at a more affordable price, recognizing that some people prefer a natural stone—even if the color is not optimum or if it has visible flaws—to a treated stone. Even more exciting, however, is the increasing interest in—and respect for—lesser-known gemstone varieties that are *not* routinely treated. Some wonderful choices are now available in a wide range of colors, including ruby red spinel, emerald green tsavorite (a green variety of garnet discovered in the 1970s), blue spinel, and fiery orange "Mandarin" garnet. A full list is provided in chapter 7. These gemstones offer beautiful, affordable, *natural* alternatives to treated gems and can usually be found at fine jewelry stores. If you have difficulty finding what you want, a gemologist or independent jeweler may be able to help you.

In short, today there are more alternatives—natural gems, treated gems, synthetic gems, and imitation gems—in more colors and more interesting designs than ever before. But the marketplace is also more complicated, and this, combined with changes in the nature of retailing itself and the increase in the number of jewelry salespeople who lack the knowledge necessary to provide reliable information and answer questions accurately, makes the situation for consumers more confusing than ever.

To help you deal with misleading or fraudulent practices, chapters that cover some of the most frequently encountered types of fraud and misrepresentation are included in this book. I want to stress, however, that the purpose is not to give you false confidence, nor is it to frighten or discourage you from buying gems and jewelry with confidence. My primary purpose in covering this material is to make you less vulnerable to the allure of fake bargains and to make you aware of the importance of buying only from knowledgeable, reputable jewelers.

Furthermore, please understand that, while information provided here may enable you to spot some fakes or detect some treatments, no book can make you an expert. Be sure to follow the advice I offer regarding what questions to ask, what to get in writing, and how to check it out to be sure of your purchase. To further pursue the field of gem identification, treatment, and enhancement, see the book *Gem Identification*

Made Easy, which is a nontechnical book for the lay person (GemStone Press, P.O. Box 237, Woodstock, VT 05091, (800) 962-4544, www.gemstonepress.com, $34.95 plus $3.75 shipping/handling).

Whatever your interest in gems, I hope they give you the pleasure and joy they have given me throughout the years. And I hope that *Colored Gemstones: The Antoinette Matlins Buying Guide* will bring greater clarity to the experience for you, and help make your gem and jewelry buying experience all that it should be: an experience filled with excitement, anticipation, romance, and pleasure.

Antoinette Matlins

Introduction

Throughout history, colored gemstones have been much sought after for their beauty, rarity, preciousness, and even "magical powers" sometimes attributed to them. They have symbolized power, wealth, and love. Every civilization, every society, grandly exhibits humankind's fascination with and desire to possess these beautiful natural creations.

We are no different from our ancestors. We too share the fascination, appreciation, and desire to possess and adorn ourselves with beautiful gemstones, and there are certainly no indicators to suggest that the allure of gems will not be as great in future generations.

Color is in vogue, even in engagement rings. Just look at London's royal family—the Queen Mother, Queen Elizabeth, Princess Anne, and Princess Diana received *sapphire* engagement rings and Princess Sarah Ferguson, a *ruby*. There has never been a more exciting time to search for a colored gem, and the experience can be a magical one. It can be filled with excitement, anticipation, and pleasure—and it is to that end that this book is dedicated.

The purpose of this book is to provide a basic but complete consumer's guide to buying a gem, whether it be for one's own personal pleasure, for a gift, or for investment in something beautiful to pass on as a treasured heirloom. It is designed and written for a wide market—husbands, wives, or parents buying gems as gifts for loved ones for some special occasion; young couples looking for an engagement ring; tourists, business travelers, and service men and women traveling throughout the world hoping to pick up gems at bargain prices while near the mines; investors looking for a hedge against inflation; and all those who are simply interested in gems as hobbyists and collectors. It will explain the variables that affect cost, provide information regarding fraudulent practices, and provide lists of relevant questions that should be asked of the seller. It will not make you a gemologist, but it will make you a more knowledgeable shopper and help transform a confusing—often frightening—experience into one that is truly interesting, exciting, and safe.

From the time I was a small child, I had the pleasure of being surrounded by beautiful gems and had a unique opportunity to learn the gem business. Having a father who was a well-known gemologist, appraiser, and collector—described as the "father of modern, practical gemology" prior to his death—I was able to spend hours marveling at stones, those in his own private collection as well as those brought to him to be professionally appraised.

Dinner conversation always centered on the day's events at my father's office. Sometimes he would thrill us with an account of a particularly fine or rare gem he had the pleasure of identifying or verifying. But too often the subject would turn to some poor, unknowing consumer who had been victimized. It might have been a soldier who thought he had purchased genuine sapphires while in Asia, who discovered sadly that they were glass or inexpensive synthetics. Or, it might have been a diplomat who had purchased jade in the Orient, only to learn it was not jade but serpentine, a common, inexpensive green stone often sold as jade. But occasionally, my father would have a wonderful story to share. One story in particular illustrates especially well how complex the gem business can be. One day an average-looking elderly woman came into my father's office with a green stone she wanted identified and appraised. She had already taken the stone to a well-known jeweler, who also had an excellent reputation as a gemologist-appraiser. The jeweler told her that the stone was a tourmaline worth only a few hundred dollars. She was very disappointed, since it was a family heirloom that she had believed for many years was a fine emerald. Her own mother had assured her of the fact. When she questioned the jeweler about its being an emerald, he laughed and told her that was impossible. He was the expert, so she accepted his appraisal, as most people would. Many months later, at the insistence of a friend who knew of my father's reputation from the curator of the Smithsonian's gem collection, she sought my father's opinion. In fact, her stone was a genuine emerald, one of the finest my father had ever seen. He could barely contain his excitement about the stone. It was worth about $60,000 even then, over 40 years ago. Fortunately, the woman learned its true identity and value before it was too late.

My first response upon hearing the story was anger at the "dishonest" jeweler, but, as my father explained, he was not dishonest. Dad actually went to see this man, because he knew his reputation was good. The jeweler discussed the stone with my father, and it became clear that he genuinely believed it to have been a tourmaline. On the basis of the woman's "ordinary" appearance and the absence of any eye-visible characteristics so typical of an emerald, he drew the immediate conclusion that the stone could only be a green tourmaline. His experience with emeralds was limited to those of lesser quality, with their telltale inclusions. His limited experience, combined with his impression of the woman, led him to make an assumption regarding the identity of the stone without even performing any definitive test. He made an incorrect identification of this unusually fine stone, but certainly he was not acting dishonestly in the hope of picking up a steal.

This anecdote illustrates the danger consumers frequently face when they come to buy gems. They are vulnerable not only to intentional fraud but also to unintentional misrepresentation resulting from a jeweler's lack of experience and knowledge. The very person on whom one would naturally rely—the jeweler—sometimes lacks sufficient knowledge about the gems he is selling. Fortunately, such educational institutions as the Gemological Institute of America (GIA), in New York and Los Angeles, and an increasing number of colleges, universities, and associations across the country that offer gemology courses, are helping to rectify this situation. More and more, reputable jewelers are concerned with increasing their own knowledge and that of their salespeople, not only to protect their valued customers but also to protect themselves!

Another incident proves how rewarding education can be. A former student of my father's was visiting in a midwestern city. She decided to go to some pawnshops to kill time, and in one shop she discovered a beautiful diamond-and-emerald ring. The pawnbroker told her that the diamonds were of an unusually fine quality, which her examination confirmed. The ring was also beautifully designed, with outstanding workmanship. Her question was whether the emerald was genuine or synthetic. As she examined the stone she began to suspect it was genuine. But she didn't have the right equipment with her to be sure. The $500 price was appropriate for the diamonds and the gold setting alone, indicating that the pawnbroker believed the emerald was synthetic. But since the visitor liked the ring, and the price was fair, she was willing to take a chance that it might in fact be genuine. Upon her return to Washington she brought the ring to my father's lab, where they proceeded immediately to examine the emerald. It was genuine. Its value was many times what she had paid; it could easily have sold for over $30,000 at a retail jewelry store. She sold it for a very handsome profit. The student profited because of her knowledge; the pawnbroker lost an opportunity because of his lack of it.

As the result of my father's long experience in the gem business, and my own professional experience, I felt that a book about gems—written just for the consumer—was desperately needed. The original edition of *Jewelry & Gems: The Buying Guide* was the first book ever written for the average gemstone consumer. This new book is based upon the fifth edition of *Jewelry & Gems: The Buying Guide,* but it focuses exclusively on colored gemstones and provides more in-depth information. The cost of gems is greater than ever before, and projections indicate that prices will continue to rise. Thus, in a market where jewelers and gem dealers are often not as knowledgeable as they should be, where the price of gems continues to rise, and where consumers consider ever more frequently buying gems for investment, the gem buyer must become more informed. A consumer cannot learn to be an expert in gems through reading a single book; a gemologist is, after all, a highly trained, skilled professional. What I can provide here is some basic information that can make buying gems a more pleasurable, less vulnerable experience.

Colored Gemstones: The Antoinette Matlins Buying Guide covers everything you, the consumer, need to know before buying any of the most popular gems. I hope you will find as much pleasure as I have found in getting to know gems, and that your future purchases will be happy ones.

Antoinette Matlins

PART  ONE

Getting to Know Gems

CHAPTER ONE

The Mystery & Magic of Colored Gems

The fascination with colored gemstones dates back to the very beginning of civilization. For our ancestors, the blue of sapphire produced visions of the heavens; the red of ruby was a reminder of the very essence of life. By Roman times, rings containing colored gems were prized symbols of power—and the most powerful wore rings on every joint of every finger!

Since ancient times, colored stones have been thought to possess innate magical powers and the ability to endow the wearer with certain attributes. According to legend, emeralds are good for the eyes; yellow stones cure jaundice; red stones stop the flow of blood. At one time it was believed that a ruby worn by a man indicated command, nobility, lordship, and vengeance; worn by a woman, however, it indicated pride, obstinacy, and haughtiness. A blue sapphire worn by a man indicated wisdom and high and magnanimous thoughts; on a woman, jealousy in love, politeness, and vigilance. The emerald signified for a man joyousness, transitory hope, and the decline of friendship; for a woman, unfounded ambition, childish delight, and change.

Colored gems, because of the magical powers associated with them, achieved extensive use as talismans and amulets, as predictors of the future, as therapeutic aids, and as essential elements to many religious practices: pagan, Hebrew, and Christian.

Zodiac Stones

The following list of the zodiacal gems and their special powers has been passed on from an early Hindu legend.

Aquarius (Jan. 21–Feb. 21)	*Garnet*—believed to guarantee true friendship when worn by an Aquarian
Pisces (Feb. 22–Mar. 21)	*Amethyst*—believed to protect a Pisces wearer from extremes of passion
Aries (Mar. 22–Apr. 20)	*Bloodstone*—believed to endow an Aries wearer with wisdom
Taurus (Apr. 21–May 21)	*Sapphire*—believed to protect from and cure mental disorders if worn by a Taurus
Gemini (May 22–June 21)	*Agate*—long life, health, and wealth were guaranteed to a Gemini if an agate ring was worn
Cancer (June 22–July 22)	*Emerald*—eternal joy was guaranteed to a Cancer-born who took an emerald along his or her way
Leo (July 23–Aug. 22)	*Onyx*—would protect a Leo wearer from loneliness and unhappiness
Virgo (Aug. 23–Sept. 22)	*Carnelian*—believed to guarantee success in anything a Virgo tried if worn on the hand
Libra (Sept. 23–Oct. 23)	*Chrysolite* (peridot)—would free a Libra wearer from any evil spell
Scorpio (Oct. 24–Nov. 21)	*Beryl*—should be worn by every Scorpio to guarantee protection from "tears of sad repentance"
Sagittarius (Nov. 22–Dec. 21)	*Topaz*—protects Sagittarians, but only if they always show the stone
Capricorn (Dec. 22–Jan. 21)	*Ruby*—a Capricorn who has ever worn a ruby will never know trouble

An old Spanish list, probably representing an Arab tradition, ascribes the following stones to the various signs of the zodiac:

Aquarius—Amethyst	*Leo*—Topaz
Pisces—(indistinguishable)	*Virgo*—Magnet (lodestone)
Aries—Crystal (quartz)	*Libra*—Jasper
Taurus—Ruby and diamond	*Scorpio*—Garnet
Gemini—Sapphire	*Sagittarius*—Emerald
Cancer—Agate and beryl	*Capricorn*—Chalcedony

The Evolution of Birthstones

The origin of the belief that a special stone was dedicated to each month, and that the stone of the month possessed a special virtue or "cure" that it could transmit to those born in that month, goes back to at least the first century. There is speculation that the twelve stones in the great breastplate of the Jewish high priest may have had some bearing on this concept. In the eighth and ninth centuries, the interpreters of the Bible's book of Revelation began to ascribe attributes of the twelve apostles to each of those stones. The Hindus, on the other hand, had their own interpretation.

But whatever the reason, one fact is clear. As G. F. Kunz points out in *The Curious Lore of Precious Stones,* "There is no doubt that the owner of a ring or ornament set with a birthstone is impressed with the idea of possessing something more intimately associated with his or her personality than any other stone, however beautiful or costly. The idea that birthstones possess a certain indefinable, but none the less real significance has long been present, and still holds a spell over the minds of all who are gifted with a touch of imagination and romance."

The following is the list of birthstones adopted in 1952 by major jewelry industry associations.

Present-Day Birthstones

Month	Birthstone	Alternative Stone
January	Garnet	
February	Amethyst	
March	Aquamarine	Bloodstone
April	Diamond	
May	Emerald	
June	Pearl	Moonstone or alexandrite
July	Ruby	
August	Sardonyx (carnelian)	Peridot
September	Sapphire	
October	Opal	Tourmaline
November	Topaz	Citrine
December	Turquoise	Lapis lazuli, zircon

Besides the lists of birthstones and zodiacal or talismanic stones, there are lists of stones for days of the week, for hours of the day, for states of the union, for each of the seasons, and even for anniversaries!

Anniversary Stones

1	Gold jewelry	13	Citrine
2	Garnet	14	Opal
3	Pearl	15	Ruby
4	Blue topaz	20	Emerald
5	Sapphire	25	Silver jubilee
6	Amethyst	30	Pearl jubilee
7	Onyx	35	Emerald
8	Tourmaline	40	Ruby
9	Lapis lazuli	45	Sapphire
10	Diamond	50	Golden jubilee
11	Turquoise	55	Alexandrite
12	Jade	60	Diamond jubilee

The Importance of Color
and Its Mystical Symbolism in Gems

The wide spectrum of color available in the gemstone realm was not lost on our forebears. Not only did strong associations with specific stones evolve, but also associations of color with personal attributes. Over time, a fairly detailed symbolism came to join color with character. Those attributes, as they have come down to us, include the following:

Yellow	Worn by a man, denotes secrecy (appropriate for a silent lover); worn by a woman, indicates generosity.
White (colorless)	Signifies friendship, integrity, and religious commitment for men; purity, affability, and contemplation for women.
Red	On a man, indicates command, nobility, lordship, and vengeance; on a woman, pride, haughtiness, and obstinacy.
Blue	On a man, indicates wisdom and high, magnanimous thoughts; on a woman, jealousy in love, politeness, vigilance.
Green	For men, signifies joyousness, transitory hope, decline of friendship; for women, unfounded ambition, childish delight, and change.
Black	For men, means gravity, good sense, constancy, and strength; for young women, fickleness and foolishness; but for married women, constant love and perseverance.
Violet	For men, signifies sober judgment, industry, and gravity; for women, high thoughts and spiritual love.

The Exciting *New* World of Gemstones— New Colors, New Gems!

Today, gems are worn primarily for their intrinsic beauty and are chosen mainly for aesthetic reasons, not for mythical attributes. While we may own a birthstone that we enjoy wearing, our choice of stones is usually dictated by personal color preferences, personal style, and economics. The fashions of the day may also influence our choices. The world of colored gems today offers us an almost endless choice. New gems have been discovered, as well as "known" gems in colors previously "unknown," and they are now taking center stage in the most important jewelry salons. If you like red, there are rubies, garnets, red tourmalines, red spinels, and even red diamonds and red "emeralds" (gemologically, red "emerald" is known as red beryl—see *Emerald* in chapter 8). If you prefer blue, there are sapphires, iolite, blue spinel, blue topaz, blue tourmaline, tanzanite, and blue diamonds. For those who prefer green, there are emeralds, tsavorite (green garnet), green zircons, green tourmalines, green sapphires, peridots, and even green diamonds. And for those who love unusual shades of blue and green, and dazzling neon shades in sparkling, transparent stones, there are the remarkable, rare, newly discovered Paraiba or Hetorita tourmalines from Brazil, considered by many to be the most exciting gemological discovery, in terms of color, in this century.

The following chapters will look at colored stones in more detail and will suggest a variety of stones available in every hue. With colored gems available for almost everyone, in almost any color, at almost any price, you have a wide range of affordable options.

CHAPTER TWO

Becoming Intimate with Gems

Gems should never be bought as a gamble—the uneducated consumer will always lose. This is a basic rule of thumb. The best way to take the gamble out of buying a particular gem is to familiarize yourself with the gem. While the average consumer can't hope to make the same precise judgments as a qualified gemologist, whose scientific training and wealth of practical experience provide a far greater database from which to operate, the consumer can learn to judge a stone as a "total personality" and learn what the critical factors are—color, clarity (also referred to in the trade as "perfection"), cut, brilliance, and weight—and how to balance them in judging the gem's value. Learning about these factors and spending time in the marketplace looking, listening, and asking questions before making the purchase will prepare you to be a wise buyer more likely to get what you really want, at a fair price.

Try to learn as much as you can about the gem you want to buy. Examine stones owned by your family and friends, and compare stones at several different jewelry stores, noting differences in shades of color, brilliance, and cut. Go to a good, established jewelry store and ask to see fine stones. If the prices vary, ask why. Let the jeweler point out differences in color, cut, or brilliance, and if he or she can't, go to another jeweler with greater expertise. Begin to develop an eye for what constitutes a fine stone by looking, listening, and asking good questions.

Here are five key questions to ask yourself before you consider buying any stone:

1. Is the color what you desire?
2. Is the shape what you want?
3. Does it have liveliness, or "zip"?
4. Do you like it and feel excited by it?
5. Can you afford it?

If you answer yes to all five questions, you are ready to examine the specific stone more carefully.

The Six Key Steps in Examining a Stone

1. *Whenever possible, examine stones unmounted.* They can be examined more thoroughly out of their settings, and defects cannot be hidden by the mounting or side stones.
2. *Make sure the gem is clean.* If you are buying a stone from a retail jeweler, ask that it be cleaned for you. If you are not in a place where it can be cleaned professionally, breathe on the stone in a huffing manner in order to steam it with your breath, and then wipe it with a clean handkerchief. This will at least remove the superficial film of grease.
3. *Hold the unmounted stone so that your fingers touch only the girdle* (the edge where top and bottom meet). Putting your fingers on the table (top) and/or pavilion (bottom) will leave traces of oil, which will affect color and brilliance.

   The *careful* use of tweezers instead of fingers is recommended only if you feel comfortable using them. Make sure you know how to use them, and get the permission of the owner before picking up the stone. It is easy for the stone to pop out of the tweezers and to become damaged or lost, and you could be held responsible.
4. *View the gem under proper lighting.* Many jewelers use numerous incandescent spotlights, usually recessed in dropped ceilings. Some use special spotlights that can make any gemstone—even glass imitations—look fantastic.

   Fluorescent lights are what professionals use for grading, but they may also adversely affect the appearance of some gems. Many red gemstones, such as rubies, look much better under incandescent light, while blue gems, such as sapphire, often look much better in daylight or fluorescent light. I recommend looking at stones in several types of light.

   The light source should come from above or behind you, shining down and through the stone, so that the light traveling through the stone is reflected back up to your eye.
5. *Rotate the stone in order to view it from different angles.*

6. *If you are using a loupe, focus it both on the surface and into the interior.* To focus into the interior, shift the stone slowly, raising or lowering it, until you focus clearly on all depths within it. This is important because if you focus on the top only, you won't see what is in the interior of the stone.

How to Use a Loupe

A loupe (pronounced *loop*) is a special type of magnifying glass. The loupe can be very helpful in many situations, even for the beginner. With a loupe you can check a stone for chips or scratches or examine certain types of noticeable inclusions more closely. Remember, however, that even with a loupe, you will not have the knowledge or skill to see or understand the many telltale indicators that an experienced jeweler or gemologist could spot. No book can provide you with that knowledge or skill. Do not allow yourself to be deluded, or let a little knowledge give you a false confidence. Nothing will more quickly alienate a reputable jeweler or mark you faster as easy prey for the disreputable dealer.

The loupe is a very practical tool to use once you master it, and with practice it will become more and more valuable. The correct type is a 10x, or ten-power, "triplet," which can be obtained from any optical supply house. The triplet type is recommended because it corrects two problems other types of magnifiers have: traces of color normally found at the outer edge of the lens, and visual distortion, also usually at the outer edge of the lens. In addition, the loupe must have a black housing around the lens, not chrome or gold, either of which might affect the color you see in the stone.

The loupe *must* be 10x because the United States Federal Trade Commission requires grading to be done under ten-power magnification. Any flaw that does not show up under 10x magnification is considered nonexistent for grading purposes.

With a few minutes' practice you can easily learn to use the loupe. Here's how:

1. Hold the loupe between the thumb and forefinger of either hand.
2. Hold the stone or jewelry similarly in the other hand.
3. Bring both hands together so that the fleshy parts just below the thumbs are pushed together and braced by the lower portion of

The loupe can tell you a great deal about the workmanship that went into cutting a gem. It can help a professional decide whether a gem is natural, synthetic, a doublet, or glass. It can provide the clues about the gem's authenticity, its durability, and its point of origin. But spotting these clues takes lots of practice and experience.

When you use a loupe, remember that you won't see what the experienced professional will see, but with a little practice, it can still be a valuable tool and might save you from a costly mistake.

CHAPTER THREE

Looking for a Gem That's a "Cut Above"

One of the most important things to learn is how to look at a gem, even if you won't see all that a gemologist will. Let's begin by making sure you understand the terms you will be hearing and using to describe what you want—especially terms pertaining to the stone's "cut" and the names for the parts of a cut stone.

It's important to be familiar with a few general terms that are commonly used in reference to faceted stones. The parts of a stone can vary in proportion and thus affect its brilliance, beauty, and desirability. This will be discussed later in greater detail.

- *Girdle.* The girdle is the edge or border of the stone that forms its perimeter; it is the edge formed where the top portion of the stone meets the bottom portion—its "dividing line." This is the part usually grasped by the prongs of a setting.
- *Crown.* The crown is also called the *top* of the stone. This is simply the upper portion of the stone: the part above the girdle.
- *Pavilion.* The pavilion is the bottom portion of the stone, the part from the girdle to the "point" at the bottom.
- *Culet.* The culet is the lowest part or point of the stone. It may be missing in some stones, which can indicate damage, or, particularly with colored stones, it may not be part of the original cut.
- *Table.* The table is the flat top of the stone and is the

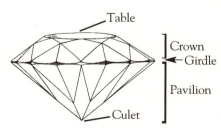

Parts of a faceted stone

15

stone's largest facet, often called the face. The term *table spread* is used to describe the width of the table facet, often expressed as a percentage of the total width of the stone.

The Cut of the Stone

The most important—and least understood—factor that must be evaluated when one considers any gem is the *cutting*. When we talk about cut, we are not referring to the shape but to the care and precision used in creating a finished gem from the rough. There are many popular shapes for gemstones. Each shape affects the overall look of the stone, but if the stone is cut well its brilliance and value endure no matter what shape it is. For the average consumer, choosing a shape is simply a matter of personal taste. Some of the most popular shapes are pictured here (new shapes are discussed in chapter 4).

Classic Shapes

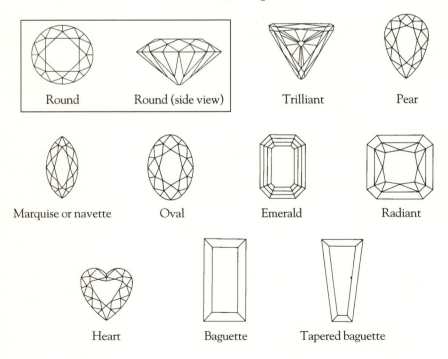

| Round | Round (side view) | Trilliant | Pear |

| Marquise or navette | Oval | Emerald | Radiant |

| Heart | Baguette | Tapered baguette |

How to Know If a Stone Is Well Cut

The precision of the cutting dramatically affects the beauty and value of any stone. This is especially true in *faceted* stones, those on which a series of tiny flat planes (facets or faces) have been cut and polished. (Nonfaceted stones are called *cabochons;* these are discussed in part 2.) By following some general guidelines and tips for looking at faceted gemstones, you can better determine both the quality of the stone and the quality of the cut.

The first thing to keep in mind is that in any stone, if the basic material is of good quality, the way it is cut will make the difference between a dull, lifeless stone and a beautiful, brilliant one. In colored gems, the perfection of the cut is not as important as it is with diamonds, but proportioning remains critical because it will significantly affect the depth of color as well as the stone's brilliance and liveliness.

Look at the stone face-up, through the top (table). This is the most critical area to view, since this is the one most often noticed. Does the color look good from this direction? Is the table centered and symmetrical?

The stone's proportion—whether it is too thin or too thick—will have a marked effect on its overall beauty. With colored stones, the relative terms of thickness or thinness vary greatly because of the inherent optical properties of different gems. As a general guide when you are considering colored stones, keep in mind these three points:

1. If the stone appears lively and exhibits an appealing color when viewed through the table, no matter how the proportion appears (thick or thin), it is usually correct and acceptable proportioning for that particular stone.
2. The depth of color (tone) will become darker as the stone is cut thicker, particularly if the bottom portion (pavilion) is deep and broad.
3. A stone's depth of color will become lighter as the stone is cut thinner. This is especially important when you are considering a pastel-colored stone. A pastel stone should always have fairly deep proportioning.

Before Beginning

As you shop for any fine gem or piece of jewelry, keep in mind the importance of visiting fine jewelry stores to look at stones and compare them. Many of the factors discussed in the following chapters will become clearer when you have actual stones before you to examine, and you will gain a deeper understanding and appreciation for the gem you are considering. Knowledgeable jewelers will also be happy to take time to help you understand differences in quality and cost.

Also keep in mind the importance of buying only from a well-trained, reputable jeweler. Remember, you are not an expert. The information provided here should help you begin your search more confidently and gain insights that will make the experience more fun, more challenging, and more fulfilling. But perhaps just as important, I hope it will help you make a wiser decision about the jeweler with whom you decide to do business, and about his or her knowledge, professionalism, and integrity. If so, this book will have provided a valuable service and perhaps saved you from a costly mistake.

PART ◆ TWO

Colored Gemstones

CHAPTER FOUR

Determining Value in Colored Gems:

What Makes a Gem a Gem?

The mention of the word *gemstone* instantly conjures up exotic images of dazzling gemstones in overflowing treasure chests or fabulous crown jewels or important museum collections. It conjures up images of dazzling color and shimmering brilliance. But the term *gemstone* or *gem* is often used carelessly to describe almost any stone. In fact, most stones are not "gems." Even among that rare group often described as "the *precious* three"—ruby, sapphire, and emerald—we find stones that are not "gems." So what is the definition of a gem?

No one has come up with a universally accepted definition, but most agree that a gemstone is a mineral (or in some cases, an organic material) that possesses unusual *beauty, durability*, and *rarity*. And I would add one more factor: it must have caché. That is, it must possess mystery, mystique, and glamour—those things that bring it into the world of our dreams and make us yearn to possess it.

While somewhat subjective, and not without some exceptions, the first three criteria are always at the heart of how we classify stones and determine whether or not they are gems. The first, and perhaps the most important, is beauty. If it isn't beautiful, why would anyone want to possess it? But beauty alone is not enough. A gem must also be sufficiently durable to withstand the normal wear and tear of use, to stand the test of time. This is at the heart of why gemstones figure so prominently as heirlooms: they are durable. It is their durability that is the key to a gem's ability to retain its beauty and allure, to be passed on from generation to generation. And finally, we must consider the rarity factor, the most important in terms of valuation. Generally speaking, the rarer the gem, the more costly, and vice versa.

Let me provide an example that might put these factors into a more relevant scenario. Several years ago I came across a number of "gemstones"—emeralds, rubies, and sapphires—that had been consigned to an auction house for sale to the highest bidder. Each stone was encased in a small folder, accompanied by a "laboratory certificate" that basically identified the stone as genuine. I watched in disbelief as each stone was sold for anywhere from $50 to $300, because not one of them was worth more than $5 (including the cost of the packaging)!

I couldn't believe anyone would be interested in bidding anything at all for these stones, because they were, above all, terribly unattractive. The bidders, however, assumed that since they were "precious gems" they were valuable. One man said that he bought them for resale because, as he explained to me, "how could he go wrong buying a three-carat emerald for $100?" He expected to sell it for several thousand dollars. He, and others like him, quickly found out how wrong they were. What they bought were not "gems" but worthless stones with no value. I suggested they might want to add them to their driveway gravel.

Let's look at why these emeralds, rubies, and sapphires were not "gems." While all of the stones were genuine, they were not "*gem*stones," because they failed to meet any of the three criteria above. First, they were not beautiful: they did not possess lovely colors, had no sparkle or liveliness, and lacked any allure whatsoever. They were plain ugly. In terms of durability, these stones had so many flaws and cracks that they probably would have broken if anyone tried to set them into a piece of jewelry (and if they did survive being placed in a piece of jewelry, they would not have survived the first week of wear). And finally, in terms of rarity, stones of such poor quality are not rare at all; they are carried away from mine sites by the ton in dump trucks. Such low-quality emeralds, rubies, and sapphires are common; they can be found all over the world, in inexhaustible quantities. There is no demand for such material, and it has no value.

Beauty, durability, and rarity are directly related to *quality* differences. Had the quality been much finer, the stones would have been more beautiful and more durable. In addition, as quality improves, rarity increases.

Rarer stones are more valuable, so the cost would have been greater. Rarity and cost are directly related, especially in cases where gemstones have immediate recognition. But today, with newly discovered gemstones, we cannot understand the impact of rarity as it relates to value without understanding the "fourth" factor: *caché.*

Let's look at one of the newest gemstones to enter the market: tsavorite. Tsavorite is a rare member of the garnet family. A fine tsavorite is one of the most beautiful gems available, occurring in a rich, deep emerald green color. It was discovered in Tsavo National Park in Kenya and introduced to the jewelry trade in the 1970s. Let's compare it to another green gem, emerald. In terms of beauty, tsavorite is more brilliant and equally beautiful (some think it even surpasses the beauty of emerald). It is also more durable, and fine-quality stones over two carats are even rarer than emerald. In terms of value, however, its cost is about one-tenth that of emerald! If beauty, durability, and rarity are the only factors to consider, why isn't tsavorite more valuable than emerald? The answer is found in the fourth factor: it lacks caché. In other words, people don't dream about owning one. At least, not yet. A gem's caché is what will ultimately affect *demand,* and demand combined with rarity is what will ultimately determine its value.

Tsavorite has a very brief history to date, less than thirty years. Other newcomers, such as red beryl (better known as *Red Emerald*™) and fiery orange Mandarin garnet, have even briefer histories. Many people have not yet even heard of them, and fewer still have seen them. All of this affects supply and demand. Currently the supply of these gems is able to meet demand. But as we move into the twenty-first century and awareness and appreciation for these wonderful—and rare—beauties increases, so will demand. And who knows, as people become more knowledgeable about the wide range of gemstone choices available, supply and demand ratios may go topsy-turvy, along with the prevailing hierarchy. Tsavorite may become the "emerald" of the twenty-first century, red spinel the "ruby" of the twenty-first century, and Paraiba tourmaline the "sapphire" of the twenty-first century. But whatever choices *you* make, the key to selecting a *gemstone,* one that will give you lasting beauty and value, lies in an understanding and appreciation for quality differences.

The Four Cs of Colored Gems

Most people are familiar with the four Cs in the context of evaluating diamond quality, but colored gemstones have four Cs of their own: color, color, color, and color! This statement may sound like an exaggeration, but not so much as you might think.

Generally speaking, the finer and rarer the color, the less impact cutting, clarity, and carat weight have on the value of the gem. On the other hand, the more common the color, the more impact these other factors have.

When we discuss color, we are not talking simply about hue. Color science and the evaluation of color constitute a very complex area. But if you understand the various elements that must be factored into the evaluation of color, you can begin to look at colored gems in a totally different light.

Color is affected by many variables that make it difficult to evaluate precisely. Perhaps the most significant factor is light; the type of light and its intensity can affect color dramatically. In addition, color can be very subjective in terms of what is considered pleasing and desirable. Nonetheless, there has been extensive research and development in the field of color science, and experts are working to develop a viable color-grading system. Gemologists at the GIA have produced a machine called *Color Master,* a type of visual colorimeter, around which they have developed a color grading system that is gaining increasing acceptance. American Gemological Laboratories has continued to develop its *ColorScan* system, and several other systems are gaining acceptance, such as *Gem Dialogue.* Many gem-pricing guides use at least one of these systems to describe the quality of the stones they are pricing, but problems still exist with color communication, and no solution seems imminent. For the time being, a great degree of subjectivity reigns where colored gems are concerned, and no system has yet replaced the age-old eye-and-brain combination, coupled with years of experience in the colored-stone field.

The Key Elements in Describing Color

The color we see in gems is always some *combination* of the pure spectral colors—which range from pure red to pure violet—coupled with varying degrees of brown, white, black, and gray. It is these latter colors, in combination with the spectral colors, that affect the *tone* of the color seen and that make the classification of color so difficult. For example, if white is present with red, you will have a lighter tone or shade of red; if black is present, a darker tone or shade. Depending on the degree of gray, white, black, or brown, an almost infinite number of color combinations can result.

As a general rule, the closer a stone's color is to the pure spectral hue, the better the color is considered to be; the closer it comes to a pure hue, the rarer and more valuable. For example, if we are considering a green stone, the purer the green, the better the color. In other words, the closer it comes to being a pure spectral green, having no undertone (tint) of any other color such as blue or yellow, the better the color. There is no such thing in nature, however, as a perfectly pure color; color is always modified by an undertone of another hue. But these undertones can create very beautiful, unusual, distinctive colors that are often very desirable.

In describing color we will often refer to these factors:

- *Hue*—the precise spectral color (red, orange, yellow, green, blue, violet, indigo)
- *Intensity* (or saturation)—the brightness or vividness (or dullness or drabness) of the color
- *Tone*—how much black, white, gray, or brown is present (how light or dark the stone is)
- *Distribution*—the even (or uneven) distribution of the color

Both the intensity and the tone of color can be significantly affected by the proportioning of the cut. In other words, a good lapidary (stone cutter) working with a fine stone will be able to bring out its inherent, potential beauty to the fullest, increasing the gem's desirability. A poor cutter may take the same rough material and create a stone that is not really pleasing, because the cut can significantly reduce the vividness and alter the depth of color, usually producing a stone that is much too dark to be attractive, or one in which the color seems washed-out or watery.

In general, stones that are either very light (pale) or very dark sell for less per carat. There seems to be a common belief that the darker the stone, the better. This is true only to a point. A rich, deep color is desirable, but not a color so deep that it appears black. The average consumer must shop around and train the eye to distinguish between a nice depth of color and a stone that is too dark.

As a general rule, it is even more important to shop around when considering colored stones than it is when buying diamonds. You must develop an eye for all of the variables of color: hue, intensity, tone, and distribution. Some stones simply exhibit a more intense, vivid color than other stones (all else being equal), but only by extensive visual comparison can you develop your eye to perceive differences and make reliable judgments.

For example, let's discuss the variations among rubies for a moment. The finest red rubies from Burma exhibit a color that, while not truly "pure red" (there may be a slight bluish undertone), comes closest to being a pure red. The tone may vary, however, from very light to very dark. As with most stones, the very light stones and the very dark sell for less per carat. Burmese rubies are the most highly prized and the most expensive because of the desirability of their color and their scarcity. They also exhibit a beautiful red in all light, while rubies from most other locations may exhibit a lovely red only in incandescent light (such as you find in candlelight, lamplight, chandeliers, and most evening light) and become pinkish or purplish when seen in fluorescent or daytime light.

Thai rubies can vary tremendously in hue and tone, going from a light to a dark red with varying degrees of a bluish undertone, giving them a purplish cast and making them look like the much cheaper reddish purple gemstone, the garnet. While some Thai rubies can have very fine color, rivaling the Burmese (these are very expensive), most Thai stones are much less expensive than the Burmese, primarily because the color can't compare.

African rubies from Tanzania usually have a tint or undertone of brown or orange, which makes them also much cheaper than the Burmese reds, but depending on the precise shade, often more valuable than the Thai ruby, depending on the latter's color. Rubies from newly discovered deposits in Kenya, Cambodia, Vietnam, Kashmir (Pakistan), and parts of China are very close in hue and tone to Burmese rubies, and may also retain their color in all light. These stones can command very high prices if other quality factors are fine.

Ceylon rubies are also encountered with relative frequency. However, these are usually paler in tone. In the United States they are called pink sapphire, not ruby, when the tone is too light. The saturation of color is too weak to be technically described as ruby, since ruby should be red, not pink. You should be aware that in the United States, the color must be deep enough to be considered red to be called ruby, while in other parts of the world, the name *ruby* may be applied if the stone falls anywhere in the pink-to-red range. (It should be noted that sapphire and ruby are the same stone, physically and chemically. The red variety is called ruby, and the equally popular blue is called sapphire. Both belong to the corundum family.)

Next, let's look at the spectrum of emerald colors. Some of the finest emeralds today come from Colombia and are the color of fresh, young green grass—an almost pure spectral green with a faint tint of either yellow or blue. Colombian emeralds owe their color to trace elements of chromium, and the color in the finest of these emeralds is unrivaled; emeralds that contain chromium are more vivid than emeralds from other locations that derive their color from trace elements of vanadium. Emeralds from other countries can also be very fine, with exceptional color, but few can match the color of the finest Colombian. Unfortunately, very fine Colombian emeralds with exceptional color are extremely rare now, and thus very costly.

Zambian emeralds can also exhibit a lovely shade of green but usually with a bluer undertone, due to traces of vanadium rather than chromium, and a slightly dark tone, probably caused by traces of iron. This color difference may make the stone less desirable and thus less valuable than a fine emerald from Colombia. However, the Zambian stones usually have fewer inclusions (flaws) than the Colombian, and cut a more vivid stone. Therefore, some of the Zambian stones, depending on depth of color, compare very favorably to the Colombian, aesthetically, while costing less per carat.

Light and Environment
Affect the Color You See

The color of a stone can be drastically affected by the kind of light and the environment in which the examination is being conducted; that is, variables as disparate as the color of the wallpaper or the tint of a shirt can alter a stone's appearance. If examined under a fluorescent light, a ruby may not show its fullest red because most fluorescent lights are weak in red rays; this causes the red in the ruby to be diminished and to appear more as a purple-red. The same ruby examined in sunlight or incandescent light (an ordinary electric lightbulb), neither of which is weak in red rays, will appear a truer, fuller red. Because the color of a ruby is dependent upon the "color temperature," or type of light used, it will always look best in warm light. A ruby looks even redder if examined against a piece of yellow-orange paper. For this reason, loose rubies are often shown in little envelopes, called parcel papers, that have a yellow-orange inner paper liner to show the red color to the fullest.

Blue sapphire, another intensely colored gem, comes in numerous tones of blue—from light to very dark, some so dark that they look black in incandescent (warm) light. Most sapphires, however, look bluest in fluorescent light, or daylight. Many contain some degree of green. The more green, the lower the price. Some even exhibit a color change—we've seen blue sapphires that were a magnificent blue in daylight turn to an amethyst purple in incandescent light. Some, like the stones from the Umba Valley in Tanzania, turn slightly lavender over time. The lighter blues are generally referred to as Ceylon-colored sapphire; the finest and most expensive blue sapphires generally come from Burma (now called Myanmar) and Kashmir and exhibit a rich, true blue in all kinds of light. Those from Kashmir exhibit a more subdued, soft, velvety look by comparison with Burmese or Ceylon-type sapphires, and are highly prized by connoisseurs.

An environment that is beneficial to your stone can also be created by the setting in which the stone is mounted. For example, an emerald-cut emerald mounted in a normal four-prong setting will not appear to have as deep a color as it will if mounted in a special box-type setting that encloses the sides of the stone. The "shadowing" effect created by this type of enclosure deepens the color of the stone. This technique, and other types of special mounting, can be used to improve the color of any colored gemstone where it is desirable to intensify the color.

Another example is found in the way imperial jade is set. A fine jade cabochon (a smooth, rounded cut that has no facets) is often mounted with a solid rim around the girdle (bezel set), with the back of the ring constructed much deeper than the actual bottom of the stone, and the back side of the ring nearly completely closed except for a small opening at the bottom center. This can improve its body color (and can also hide a stone's defect).

Opal, too, is often set in ways that enhance color. The environment in this case is a closed, flat backing, which has been blackened on the inside. By contrast against the black background, the play of color (fire) seen in the stone is intensified.

A Word about Color Distribution, or Zoning

Even though zoning doesn't really describe color, and is sometimes evaluated as part of the clarity grade, I think it should be discussed as part of color evaluation.

In some stones, the color isn't always evenly distributed but exists in *zones;* in some stones, the pattern created by alternating zones of color and colorlessness resembles stripes. Zoning is frequently observed in amethyst, ruby, and sapphire. These zones are most easily seen if you look through the side of the stone and move it slowly, while tilting and rotating it.

Zones of color
in a stone

Sometimes a stone in the rough is colorless, or nearly so, but has a spot or layer of color. If the cutter cuts the stone so that the culet is in the color spot, the whole stone will appear that color. If there is a layer and the cutter cuts the stone so that the layer lies in a plane nearly parallel to the table, the whole stone will look completely colored. Evenness of color and complete saturation of color are very important in determining the value of colored gems. Even though you may not notice the zones themselves when looking at the stone from the top, a heavily zoned stone will lack the color vibrancy of another stone without such zoning. Normally, if the zoning isn't noticeable from the top, value is not dramatically reduced, but a stone with even color will appear more vivid from the top—the face-up position, as seen when mounted—and will cost more. And, depending upon the hue and tone, possibly much more.

A Word about Color-Change Stones

Some stones exhibit a very strange phenomenon when viewed in different types of light: they change color completely. These stones are called color-change gems. There are color-change spinels, color-change sapphires, color-change garnets, and even color-change tourmalines! In these gem families, however, the color change phenomenon is rare. The gem alexandrite, on the other hand, *always* exhibits a color change, and its value is based largely on the degree of change. There are even color-change synthetics, such as the inexpensive synthetic color-change sapphire that is often misrepresented and sold as genuine alexandrite. Alexandrite is a bluish green gem in daylight or under daylight-type fluorescent light, and a deep red or purple-red under incandescent light.

What is Fluorescence?

Fluorescence, a form of luminescence, is a property that some gemstones have that causes the stone to show a distinct color when exposed to ultraviolet rays produced by an ultraviolet lamp. The color of a stone viewed under ultraviolet rays can be a more intense shade of the stone's normal body color or an altogether different color. If you have ever visited a museum and seen common, drab-colored rocks suddenly light up in psychedelic colors when the room is darkened and the "black light" (a type of ultraviolet light) is turned on, then you have seen this phenomenon known as "fluorescence." These minerals appear to be a certain color when seen in normal light, but when viewed under pure ultraviolet wavelengths, they reveal altogether different colors.

Ultraviolet rays are all around us. They are present in daylight (sunburn is caused by certain ultraviolet wavelengths) and in those long tubes that give us "fluorescent" light (but a different wavelength is emitted that is not harmful and does not cause sunburn). An *ultraviolet lamp* produces only ultraviolet radiation—long-wave ultraviolet and short-wave ultraviolet—and a gemstone's reaction to ultraviolet radiation can be an important key to gemstone identification and treatment detection.

Fluorescence is one of nature's most interesting phenomena to observe. However, ultraviolet radiation and its ability to stimulate fluorescence in gemstones is really not difficult to understand. You simply need to know that there is visible light and invisible light all around us. Light travels in waves, and the length of those waves determines whether they are *visible* or *invisible*, and what color we actually see. Some light waves are too short to be visible to humans; some are too long to be visible. The colors we see—red, orange, yellow, green, blue, and violet—

have wavelengths that occur in a range visible to the human eye. Ultraviolet has wavelengths that go beyond violet, and are outside our visible range, so they are invisible to us.

Rays produced by an ultraviolet lamp are too short for us to see, but when they strike certain gems, properties within those gems *change the length of the invisible wavelengths into longer wavelengths so that they become visible.* When this happens, colors appear that were not visible before viewing with the ultraviolet lamp. When a gemstone produces colors that can be seen only with the ultraviolet lamp, we say it *fluoresces* or it has *fluorescence.* Some stones fluoresce only under long-wave ultraviolet radiation, some only under short-wave, and some fluoresce under both wavelengths but show a stronger reaction under one wavelength than the other. Whether or not a stone fluoresces, the particular colors in which it fluoresces, and the wavelength under which it fluoresces—long-wave or short-wave—is important to note and will be indicated on any colored gemstone report.

Fluorescence Can Affect the Color Seen in Different Lighting Environments

As mentioned earlier, fluorescence is an important key to the identification of many gemstones and can also be indicative of certain types of treatment. But even more important, it can affect the color we see in daylight and a stone's color trueness in all types of lighting. This is the case with Burmese ruby, for example. One of the characteristics that make ruby of Burmese origin so desirable is its fluorescence. Burmese rubies fluoresce red under short-wave, and very strong red under long-wave, whereas most Thai rubies have a very weak to inert fluorescence and this can affect the color we perceive in different lighting environments. Thai rubies and Burma rubies will both show a nice red color in "incandescent" light (a warm light in which any red stone looks great), but a Thai ruby will look much *less* red in daylight, whereas the Burma ruby—which fluoresces a good red under all ultraviolet wavelengths—will still show a good red in daylight because of the ultraviolet radiation present naturally in daylight!

Clarity

As with diamonds, *clarity* refers to the absence of internal flaws (inclusions) or external blemishes. Flawlessness in colored stones is perhaps even rarer than in diamonds. However, while clarity is important, and the cleaner the stone the better, flawlessness in colored stones does not usually carry the premium that it does with diamonds. Light, pastel-colored stones will require better clarity because the flaws are more readily visible in these stones; in darker-toned stones, the flaws may not be as important a variable because they are masked by the depth of color.

The *type* and *placement* of flaws is a more important consideration in colored stones than the presence of flaws in and of themselves. For example, a large crack (also called a *fracture* or *feather)* that is very close to the surface of a stone—especially on the top—might be dangerous because it weakens the stone's durability. It may also break the light continuity, and may show an iridescent effect as well (iridescence usually means that a fracture or feather breaks through the surface somewhere on the stone). Such a large crack would detract from the stone's beauty and certainly reduce its value. But if the fracture is small and positioned in an unobtrusive part of the stone, it will have minimal effect on durability, beauty, or value. Some flaws actually help a gemologist or jeweler to identify a stone, since certain types of flaws are characteristic of specific gems and specific localities. In some cases, a particular flaw may provide positive identification of the exact variety or origin and actually cause an increase in the per-carat value. For more information on the types of inclusions found in colored gems, I recommend the book *Gem Identification Made Easy.* I should note, however, that a very fine colored gem that really is flawless will probably bring a disproportionately *much* higher price per carat because it is so rare. Because they are so rare, flawless rubies, sapphires, emeralds, and so on should always be viewed with suspicion; have their genuineness verified by a gem-testing lab. The newer synthetic gems are often flawless and are easy to confuse with genuine, natural gems.

If the flaws weaken the stone's durability, affect color, are easily noticeable, or are too numerous, they will significantly reduce price. Otherwise, they may not adversely affect price, and in some cases, if they provide positive identification and proof of origin, they may actually increase the cost rather than reduce it. Such is the case with Burmese rubies and Colombian emeralds.

Again, it is important to shop around, become familiar with the stone you wish to purchase, and train your eye to discern what is "normal" so you can decide what is acceptable or objectionable.

Terms Used to Describe Optical Effects in Faceted and Nonfaceted Gems

The physical characteristics of colored stones are often described in terms of the way light travels through them, their unique visual effects, and the way they are cut. Here are a few terms you need to know:

- *Transparent.* Light travels through the stone easily, with minimal distortion, enabling one to see through it easily.
- *Translucent.* The stone transmits light but diffuses it, creating an effect like frosted glass. If you tried to read through such a stone, the print will be darkened and obscured.
- *Opaque.* The stone transmits no light; you cannot see through it even at a thin edge.

Special Optical Effects

- *Adularescence.* A billowy, movable cloud effect seen in some stones, such as moonstone; an internal, movable sheen.
- *Asterism.* Used to describe the display of a star effect (four- or six-rayed) seen when a stone is cut in a nonfaceted style (star ruby, garnet, and sapphire.)
- *Chatoyancy.* The effect produced in some stones (when cut in a cabochon style) of a thin, bright line across the stone that usually moves as the stone is moved from side to side; sometimes called a *cat's-eye* effect.
- *Iridescence.* A rainbow color effect produced by a thin film of air or liquid within the stone. Most iridescence seen in stones is the result of a crack breaking the surface. This detracts from the value, even if it looks pretty.
- *Luster.* Usually refers to the surface of a stone and the degree

to which it reflects light. Seen as the shine on the stone. Diamond, for example, has much greater luster than amethyst. Pearls are also evaluated for their luster, but pearls have a softer, silkier-looking reflection than other gems. The luster in pearls is often called orient.

• *Play of color.* Used frequently to describe the fire seen in opal, or the multiple flashes or pattern of color.

Cut

Colored gems can be either *faceted* or cut in a *nonfaceted* style called *cabochon*. Generally speaking, the preference in the United States until recently was for faceted gems, so the finest material was usually faceted. However, this was not always the case in other eras and other countries. In Roman times, for example, it was considered vulgar to wear a faceted stone. Preference also varies with different cultures and religions, and the world's finest gems are cut in both styles. Don't draw any conclusions about quality based solely on style of cut.

Cabochon cut
Note the smooth top of this *sugarloaf* cabochon.

Cabochon. A facetless style of cutting that produces a smooth surface. These cuts can be almost any shape. Some are round with high domes; others look like squarish domes (the popular "sugarloaf" cabochon); others are "buff-topped," showing a somewhat flattened top.

Many people around the world prefer the quieter, often more mysterious personality of the cabochon. Some connoisseurs believe that cabochons produce a richer color. Whatever the case, today we are seeing much more interest in and appreciation for cabochons around the world, and more beautiful cabochons than have been seen in the market in many years.

Faceted. A style of cutting that consists of giving to the stone many small faces at varying angles to one another, as in various diamond cuts. The placement, angle, and shape of the faces, or facets, is carefully planned and executed to show the stone's inherent beauty—fire, color, brilliance—to fullest advantage. Today there are many "new" faceted styles, including "fantasy" cuts, which combine rounded surfaces with sculpted backs.

The Importance of Cut

As stated earlier, cutting and proportioning in colored stones are important for two main reasons: they affect the *depth* of color seen in the stone; and they affect the *liveliness* projected by the stone.

Color and cutting are the most important criteria in determining the beauty of a colored stone. After that, carat weight must be factored in; the higher carat weight will usually increase the price per carat, generally in a nonlinear proportion. If a colored stone was of a good-quality material to begin with, a good cut will enhance its natural beauty to the fullest and allow it to exhibit its finest color and liveliness. If the same material is cut poorly, its natural beauty will be lessened, causing it to look dark, too light, or even "dead."

Therefore, when you examine a colored stone that looks lively to your eye and has good color—not too dark and not too pale—you can assume the cut is reasonably good. If the stone's color is poor, or if it lacks liveliness, you must examine it for proper cut. If it has been cut properly, you can assume the basic material was poor. If the cut is poor, however, the material may be very good and can perhaps be recut into a beautiful gem. In this case you may want to confer with a knowledgeable cutter to see if it is worthwhile to recut, considering cutting costs and loss in weight. If you don't know any cutters, a reputable jeweler, gemologist-appraiser, or local lapidary club may be able to recommend one.

Evaluating the Cut of a Colored Gem

When you are examining the stone for proper cut, a few considerations should guide you:

Is the shade pleasing, and does the stone have life and brilliance? If the answer is yes to both questions, then the basic material is probably good, and you must make a decision based on your own personal preferences and budget.

Is the color too light or too dark? If so, and if the cut looks good, the basic uncut material was probably too light or too dark to begin with. Consider purchase only if you find the stone pleasing, and only if the price is right, i.e., significantly lower than stones of better color.

Is the stone's brilliance even, or are there dead spots or flat areas? Often the brilliance in a colored gemstone is not uniform. If the color is exceptional, subdued brilliance may not have a dramatic effect on its allure, desirability, or value. However, the less fine the color, the more important brilliance becomes.

When the cut is not properly proportioned a stone can either look too dark or too light. In other cases, a cut can mask the fact that a stone has little color. When evaluating the cut of a stone, here are some additional considerations:

When the color is too dark. This is usually the case if the proportioning is too thick or deep. In a thick stone, it is possible that the original material was of good color tone and that poor cutting created the undesirable darkness. The cost of this stone should be less per carat than one less dark, and it may, therefore, be feasible to purchase it (if the price is sufficiently low) and invest in recutting the stone to better proportions to enhance its natural color. While the size or weight would be reduced, the price per carat would be increased. At worst, there would be a tradeoff: reduced size for increased beauty and increased price per carat. In some cases the price per carat may increase so substantially that the overall value of the stone also increases substantially, even though it weighs less.

This is often the case with "native cut" stones, a term used in the trade to describe stones cut by less skilled workers who are cutting with only one goal in mind: to get the heaviest stone possible. These stones are usually too deep and therefore look thick, heavy, very dark, and often lifeless. While many of these stones are undesirable in their "native cuts," they can often be recut into lively stones with a much more pleasing color and greater beauty and desirability. In such cases, the price per carat increases, resulting in a stone that may be more valuable than the larger stone before recutting.

When the color is too light. The basic color of the gemstone may simply be light in tone, but it may also be the result of poor proportioning from having been cut too shallow. Shallow stones usually lack liveliness, but it is usually not feasible to recut them.

A stone that is cut too shallow may also be more vulnerable to breakage. Some stones are so shallow that they really should not be worn at all or, if so, only in a piece of jewelry that will be protected and less exposed to the normal knocks and blows of everyday wear.

In shallow-cut pastel or light-colored stones, such as aquamarine, amethyst, or topaz, any accumulation of dirt or grease on the back of the stone will more quickly and dramatically diminish color and brilliance. This often happens with a ring worn daily and subjected to dishwashing, cosmetic application, bath oils, etc. To remain attractive, pastel or light-colored stones should be frequently cleaned (see chapter 12), especially when cut shallow.

You must also keep in mind that a gemstone is often cut in a particular way because of *where the color occurs within the stone.* As mentioned earlier, nature doesn't often create gemstones with the color evenly and uniformly distributed. Color often occurs in zones and the cutter must be sure that he or she doesn't cut the stone in a way that removes the color zone. This often affects the depth of the cut.

While gemstones are usually cut deep in an effort to get the heaviest stone possible, or to darken the tone if too light, there is another situation that you may encounter in colored gemstones—one that can cause a costly mistake. *A virtually colorless stone can appear to have color throughout if the cutter is able to capture a zone of color in the right part of the stone.* I've seen sapphires, for example, that were actually colorless, except for a tiny spot of color at the culet. One of the best bluff stones I've ever seen was a three-carat round blue sapphire that was cut very deep. For its weight it was small, so I looked more carefully from the side and back, only to discover that the stone had no blue at all except for a very tiny zone just above the culet. The entire stone looked blue because of the way the light traveled through it. The reflected light created the impression that the color was evenly distributed throughout the stone. It looked like a decent blue sapphire when viewed face-up in the mounting, but on closer examination it became immediately clear that it was not as fine as it appeared, and worth much less than the asking price.

Tip: always turn the stone onto its table, against a white or light background, and view it carefully through the sides, while gently tilting and rotating the stone to see where the color is actually located. This can be done even with mounted stones.

Gemstones are usually cut deeper to improve the tone, but sometimes the tone or overall appearance is improved by cutting the stone shallow. Sometimes a stone will be cut on the shallow side because the basic color is very deep, perhaps overly deep, and it will appear too dark if cut to a more standard depth. In other cases, a stone might have to be cut shallow to eliminate unsightly inclusions, and the cutter must hope that the finished stone won't be too pale. If the inherent color is not very rich to start, shallow cutting will result in a stone that will be too pale; if the inherent color is very rich, the color may still appear very fine regardless of its shallow cut. If it is not cut overly shallow, it may still be very desirable and still exhibit a good liveliness. I recall a lovely ruby that had belonged to an important family in India. The stone weighed just over eleven carats, but it appeared much larger. Its measurements were actually larger than an eighteen-carat ruby in another jewel. The cut was shallow, but the color was nonetheless very rich. The stone had a very mysterious personality, and the overall effect was one of great allure. It is also worth noting that the inherent color of the rough gem had to have been exceptional to have retained such color in a shallow stone.

When evaluating the cut of a colored gemstone, always pay special attention to its depth and the impact of the depth on the basic body color and overall liveliness and brilliance. Keep in mind, however, that there are exciting new cutting techniques (see below) that can create intense color and liveliness within stones that once would have been considered too shallow. Remember that the most important thing about the cutting and proportioning of any colored gemstone is the end result—its beauty. For this, the best test is simply your own eye.

Artists in Stone—The Art of Lapidary

Lapidary is the term used for gem cutting and gem cutters. The art of lapidary—fashioning a piece of "rough" stone or crystal into a sparkling gem that will dazzle the eye—is thousands of years old. For colored gemstones, one of the most famous lapidary centers is Idar Oberstein in Germany, which has been a leading lapidary center for centuries. Famous in Roman times, it has continued into the present as a major cutting center, virtually without interruption. It continues to produce some of the finest cutters, carvers, and cutting innovations, such as the first "fantasy" cut created by Bernd Münsteiner, a well-known cutter in Idar.

Lapidary has evolved as an art form over the centuries, but it is really only within the past few decades that it has moved to center stage. Today, science and technology have provided cutters and carvers with the means to experiment with new approaches and techniques that have enabled them to reach new heights in their art. There is greater knowledge about how light moves within each gemstone and, perhaps even more important, how various cutting and carving techniques can affect the *behavior* of the light. As a result, lapidary artists are now creating visual effects never imagined—new dimensions that truly represent "art" in every sense.

Lapidary artists use gemstones as the medium in which they work, often studying the material for weeks or months before deciding how to proceed. Their work is distinctive and recognizable, and the skill and artistry they bring to the fashioning of the gemstone material not only enhances its beauty and desirability but also its value. Just as a painting is valued at more than the cost of the paint and canvas, so it is with gemstones; a magnificently cut gemstone is valued not just for its weight, color, and clarity, but for the beauty added by the cutter. The value of an exquisitely cut gem is much greater than one that is cut in a more common manner.

We now see the work of lapidary artists in breathtaking jewels, magnificent sculptures, objets d'art, and, in some cases, works that combine all three in a single creation. In recent years the work of some of the most important contemporary lapidary artists has been on exhibition at such revered institutions as the Smithsonian Institution in Washington, D.C., the Carnegie Museum of Natural History in Pittsburgh, and the Field Museum in Chicago. (See color insert.)

The lapidary artist faces challenges unknown to artists working in other media. If they are to achieve the desired result, lapidary artists must constantly assess and reassess numerous elements—color, and where it occurs within the gemstone; light refraction; light reflection; the presence and placement of inclusions; and the shape of the rough. For some lapidary artists, this is doubly demanding because their work incorporates more than one gemstone material within the same piece. But even more challenging, the lapidary artist cannot ignore the intrinsic value of the gemstone material with which he or she is working. Mistakes can be very costly; the cost of canvas and oil is one thing, but the cost of a gemstone is quite another!

In addition to the risk of breaking or damaging a gem, creating maximum beauty usually means sacrificing the size of the finished gem and committing much more time to its creation. Many cutters cut the rough with one aim only: getting the largest possible size, and doing it as quickly as possible. But the goal of the lapidary artist is very different; the goal is to create the most beautiful gem possible, one that is unique, distinctive, and memorable.

Innovative Cutting Techniques
Change the World of Colored Gemstones

In traditional faceting, the primary goal of the cutter is to maximize the *brilliance* of a gemstone, the amount of light coming back *out* of the stone, back to the eye. The cutter must take into consideration the gemstone's *refractive index* (RI)—a number that indicates how light travels within the gemstone and provides a key to its relative brilliance. The higher the RI, the higher the brilliance can be; the lower the RI, the lower the brilliance. Every gem has a unique refractive index. Ruby, for example, has an RI of approximately 1.76–1.77, which is high; amethyst has an RI of approximately 1.54, which is much lower. This means that ruby has a much higher inherent brilliance factor than amethyst. So, if both stones were cut in the same manner, with the same proportions, angles, and so on, the ruby would be much more brilliant than the amethyst. Some of the earliest faceting innovations dealt with ways to get greater brilliance out of gemstones with lower RIs, that is, to get more light reflecting back out of the stone. Thus began experimentation with the shape, number, and placement of flat faces on the surface of the gemstone material, resulting in many exquisitely brilliant gemstones. Until recently, however, the techniques used involved conventional *flat* faceting, and the focus always remained on increasing the amount of light being reflected back and creating more intense brilliance.

Today's lapidary artists have introduced a whole new style of cutting with a totally different focus. The focus is no longer confined to how much light is coming *out* of the gemstone but on what is happening to the light *within* the gemstone. We are now seeing sculpturing techniques applied to this end, and some carvers have developed a unique style that involves the delicate carving of narrow "passageways" into the interior of a stone to alter the path of the light. But perhaps the most important development is in the faceting arena. Focusing on internal performance has led to a much more difficult and complex form of faceting: *curved* faceting. Using a combination of *concave* and *convex* facets, sometimes in conjunction with flat faceting and sculpturing techniques, the cutter's goal is now on using the stone's unique RI—the unique way in which light will behave when traveling through it—to capture the inner dimension and personality of the gem. Today the lapidary artist seeks to use the gemstone's own unique optical properties to create a unique interaction of color, brightness, and luminosity to reveal the inner world of the gem. These innovative techniques have resulted in some of the most beautiful gemstones ever imagined, gemstones that are truly as nature intended—one-of-a-kind.

We are now seeing incredible works by very gifted cutters and carvers, encouraged by international cutting competitions such as the *Cutting Edge Awards* sponsored by the American Gem Trade Association and, in Idar Oberstein, Germany, *The German Award for Jewelry and Precious Stones* sponsored by the Federal Association of the Precious Stones and Diamond Industry and Industrial Association for Jewelry and Metalware. Some of the best-known award winners include Susan Allen, Stephen Avery, David Brackna, Michael Christy, Michael Dyber, Mark Gronlund, Richard Homer, Martin Key, Dieter Lorenz, Thomas McPhee, Nicolai Medvedev, Bernd Münsteiner, Thomas Trozzo, Steve Walters, Larry Winn, and Phil Youngman. Each has played a significant role in creating new ways to reveal the maximum beauty of gemstones (see the color insert for examples of their work).

Weight

As with diamonds, weight in colored stones is measured in carats. All gems are weighed in carats, except pearls and coral. These materials are sold by the grain, momme, and millimeter. A grain is ¼ of a carat; a momme is 18¾ carats. Since 1913, most countries have agreed that a carat weighs 200 milligrams, or ⅕ of a gram. This carat is sometimes referred to as the *metric carat.*

Before 1913, the carat weight varied depending on the country of origin—the Indian carat didn't weigh the same as the English carat; the French carat was different from the Indian or the English. This is important if you have, or are thinking of buying, a very old piece that still has the original bill of sale indicating carat weight; the old carat weighed *more* than the post-1913 metric carat. Therefore, an old three-carat stone will weigh more than three carats by modern standards.

The carat is a unit of weight, *not size*. I wish to stress this point, since most people think that a one-carat stone is a particular size. Most people, therefore, would expect a one-carat diamond and a one-carat emerald, for example, to look the same size or to have the same apparent dimensions. This is not the case.

Comparing a one-carat diamond with a one-carat emerald and a one-carat ruby easily illustrates this point. First, emerald weighs less than diamond, and ruby weighs more than diamond. This means that a one-carat emerald will look larger than a one-carat diamond, while the ruby will look smaller than a diamond of the same weight. Emerald, with a mineral composition that is lighter, will yield greater mass per carat; ruby, with its heavier composition, will yield less mass per carat.

Let's look at the principle another way. If you compare a one-inch cube of pine wood, a one-inch cube of aluminum, and a one-inch cube of iron, you would easily choose the cube of iron as heaviest, even though it has the same *volume* as the other materials. The iron is like the ruby, while the wood is like the emerald and the aluminum like the diamond. Equal *volumes* of different materials can have very different weights depending on their *density*, also called *mass* or *specific gravity* (S.G.).

Each gemstone has its own unique specific gravity, a number that shows the ratio of the weight of the particular gem to the weight of an equal volume of water. The higher a gem's specific gravity, the heavier the gem; the lower the specific gravity, the lighter the gem (see chapter 8).

Equal volumes of materials with the same density should have approximately the same weight, so that in diamond, the carat weight has come to represent particular sizes. But these sizes are based on diamonds always being cut to more or less the same proportions. Consequently, diamonds of a particular weight will always be more or less the same size; a one-carat round diamond is always approximately 6.5 millimeters in diameter; a two-carat round diamond is always approximately 8.2 millimeters in diameter, and so on. *But these sizes do not apply to other gems.*

As a result of the close association between diamond weights and sizes, when most people describe the size gemstone they want in terms of carat weight, they are visualizing a size that is related to diamonds. For example, when someone says that they want a one-carat round sapphire, what they usually mean is that they want a sapphire that looks the *size* of a one-carat diamond—something about 6.5 millimeters in diameter.

In addition to the density of a particular gemstone affecting its size, the size of colored gemstones can be dramatically affected by the cutting. As mentioned earlier, sometimes the cutter just wants the heaviest carat weight possible and cuts a stone overly deep; it may weigh a lot, but if all the weight is in the bottom of the stone, it can look smaller than another stone that weighs half as much. Sometimes a stone is cut overly shallow in an attempt to lighten the color tone, which can create a larger-looking stone than one of the same weight with a deeper cut. Whatever the case, the proportions will affect the finished "size" of the stone.

With colored gemstones, rather than asking for a specific carat weight, it is better to show the jeweler the approximate *size* you want, perhaps using a diamond as a reference. Just remember that if you use a diamond as a reference size-wise, ask the jeweler to give you that stone's *millimeter dimensions* (the diameter or length and width), not the carat weight, so that you know what size you are seeking.

Normally, the greater the weight, the greater the value per carat, unless the stones reach unusually large sizes, for example, in excess of 50 carats. At that point, size may become prohibitive for use in some types of jewelry (rings or earrings), selling such large stones can be difficult, and price per carat may drop. There are genuine cut topazes, weighing from 2,500 to 12,000 carats, which could be used as paperweights.

Some stones are readily available in large sizes; tourmaline, for example, often occurs in stones over 10 carats. For other stones, sizes over 5 carats may be very rare and therefore considered large, and will also command a proportionately higher price. Examples include precious topaz, alexandrite, demantoid and tsavorite garnets, ruby, and red beryl. With gems that are rare in large sizes, a 10-carat stone can command any price—a king's ransom. A 30-carat blue diamond was sold in 1982 for $9 million. Today, $9 million would be considered a bargain for that stone!

Scarcity of certain sizes among the different colored stones affects the definition of *large* in the colored-gem market. A fine 5-carat alexandrite or ruby is a very large stone; an 18-carat tourmaline is a "nice size."

As with diamonds, stones under 1 carat sell for less per carat than stones over 1 carat. But here it becomes more complicated. The definition of large or rare sizes differs tremendously, as does price, depending on the type of stone. For example, an 8-carat tourmaline is an average-size stone, fairly common, and will be priced accordingly. A 5-carat tsavorite is extremely rare, and will command a price proportionately much greater than a 1-carat stone. Precious topaz used to be readily available in 20-carat sizes and larger, but today even 10-carat stones of very fine color are practically nonexistent, and their price has jumped tremendously.

The chart of colored gemstones in chapter 7 indicates the availability of stones in large sizes; and it shows where scarcity may exist, and at what size.

Colored Gemstone Certificates

Systems for grading colored gemstones are not yet established world-wide. As a result, certificates or grading reports for colored gemstones vary widely in the information provided. Reports for colored stones have a more limited value in some respects than diamond reports, which are widely relied on to describe and confirm diamond quality using precise, universally accepted standards. Nonetheless they are *very* important.

Today's new-type synthetics, newly discovered gemstone materials, and increased use of treatments are creating a need for reports that verify *identity* (the type of gem), *genuineness* (whether it is synthetic or not), whether *natural* or *treated,* and, if treated, the *type* and *degree of treatment.*

If considering the purchase of any expensive colored gemstone today, especially gems of unusual size or exceptional quality and rarity, I recommend obtaining a report from a recognized laboratory (see appendix). The most widely recognized reports for colored gemstones include those issued in the United States by American Gemological Laboratories (AGL), Gemological Institute of America (GIA) Gem Trade Laboratory, and American Gem Trade Association (AGTA) Gemological Testing Center; in Switzerland, leading firms are Laboratory Gübelin and Schweizerische Stiftung für Edelstein-Forschung (SSEF); in the United Kingdom, the Gemmological Association and Gem Testing Laboratory of Great Britain; in Belgium, Hoge Raad voor Diamant (HRD).

At the least, colored gemstone reports should identify the gemstone and verify whether it is natural or synthetic. You can also request a *grading report,* which will provide, in addition to identity, a full description of the stone and a rating of the color, clarity, brilliance, and other important characteristics. Just keep in mind that there is no universally accepted grading system, so each lab uses its own. Nonetheless, they provide important information pertaining to the stone's quality. This information is always useful for insurance purposes and can also be helpful if you are comparing several stones with an eye toward purchase. Also, depending on the information the gemologist can obtain from the gemstone during examination, some laboratories will indicate country of origin, if requested. The AGL, the AGTA Lab, SSEF, and Laboratory Gübelin will indicate origin when possible; GIA will not indicate country of origin.

Treatment disclosure is essential. Whether or not a gem has been treated and, if so, the degree of treatment, affect value and durability as well as appearance. Furthermore, it is important to know whether or not the treatment is permanent and whether it necessitates special care. Regardless of the type of report, treatment information should be included. *"Quality" or "origin" reports that omit information related to treatments are insufficient to make sound decisions.*

In the past few years we have begun to see "treatment" or "enhancement" reports. These reports confirm identity and genuineness and also include important information pertaining to treatments. They indicate whether or not the color and clarity have been enhanced. In addition, they include the degree of enhancement—such as faint, moderate, extensive, or a similar description. In some cases, the report will indicate the type of treatment or filler if there are sufficient gemological data, but sometimes these data are not available without very sophisticated equipment that many labs do not have. An "enhancement" report alone is often sufficient to make a purchase decision, since your own eye may be able to provide the rest of the information you need—especially if you have taken sufficient time to look at and compare lots of stones.

Fees for colored gemstone reports vary depending on the type of gem; the type of report requested; and the time, skill, and gemological equipment necessary to perform conclusive tests. An estimate can usually be obtained by making a telephone call to the laboratory. When you are considering a colored gemstone that is accompanied by a report, keep in mind the different types of reports available. Also keep in mind that the information provided on the report is only as reliable as the gemologist performing the evaluation, so be sure the report is issued by a respected laboratory; if in doubt, check with one of the labs listed in the appendix to see if they are familiar with the laboratory in question. Next, ask yourself what the report is really telling you—is it confirming identity and genuineness only? If so, remember that *quality* differences determine value—a genuine one-carat ruby, sapphire, or emerald can sell for $10 or $10,000 or more, depending on the quality of the particular stone. *Being genuine doesn't mean a stone is valuable.*

Take time to look at many stones, ask questions, and make comparisons. In this way you can develop a good eye and an understanding of the differences that affect quality rating, beauty, and value.

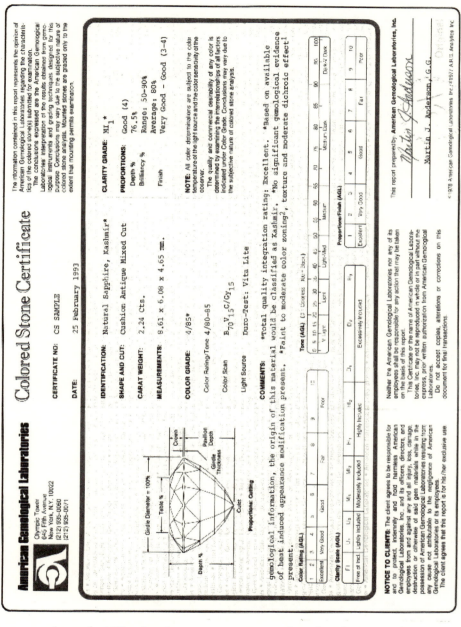

American Gemological Laboratories

Olympic Tower
645 Fifth Avenue
New York, N.Y. 10022
(212) 935-0060
(212) 935-0071

Colored Stone Certificate

CERTIFICATE NO: CS SAMPLE

DATE: 25 February 1993

IDENTIFICATION: Natural Sapphire, Kashmir*

SHAPE AND CUT: Cushion Antique Mixed Cut

CARAT WEIGHT: 2.24 Cts.

MEASUREMENTS: 8.61 x 6.08 x 4.65 mm.

COLOR GRADE: 4/85*

Color Rating/Tone 4/80-85

Color Scan $B_{70}V_{15}G/Gy_{15}$

Light Source Duro-Test: Vita Lite

COMMENTS: *Total quality integration rating: Excellent. *Based on available gemological information, the origin of this material would be classified as Kashmir. *No significant gemological evidence of heat induced appearance modification present. *Faint to moderate color zoning², texture and moderate dichroic effect¹ present.

CLARITY GRADE: MI_1*

PROPORTIONS:
Depth % 76.5%
Brilliancy % Range: 50-90%
Average: 80%
Finish Very Good - Good (3-4)

NOTE: All color determinations are subject to the color temperature of the light source and the color sensitivity of the observer.

The quality and commercial desirability of any color is determined by examining the interrelationships of all factors indicated under Color Grade. Conclusions may vary due to the subjective nature of colored stone analysis.

The information contained in this report represents the opinion of American Gemological Laboratories regarding the characteristics of the colored stone(s) submitted for examination.

The conclusions expressed are the American Gemological Laboratories' interpretation of the results obtained from gemological instruments and grading techniques designed for this purpose. Conclusions may vary due to the subjective nature of colored stone analysis. Mounted stones are graded only to the extent that mounting permits examination.

Color Rating (AGL)

1	2	3	4	5	6	7	8	9	10
Excellent	Very Good		Good			Fair			Poor

Clarity Scale (AGL)

F1	I1	L2	L3	Mi1	Mi2	Hi1	Hi2	
Free of incl.	Lightly Included			Moderately Included			Highly Included	

Tone (AGL)

0	5	10	15	20	25	30	35	40	45	50	55	60	...
C	Colorless	V. Lgt					Light			Light/Med		Medium	Excessively Included

Proportions/Finish (AGL)

1	2	3	4	5	6	7	8	9	10
Excellent		Very Good		Good			Fair		Poor
		55			75	80	85	90	95	100

Girdle Diameter = 100%

Table %

Crown

Pavilion Depth

Girdle Thickness

Culet

Depth %

Proportions: Cutting

This report prepared by **American Gemological Laboratories, Inc.**

Martin J. Anderson, G.G.

©1978 American Gemological Laboratories Inc.

NOTICE TO CLIENTS: The client agrees to be responsible for and to protect, indemnify and hold harmless American Gemological Laboratories, Inc. and its officers, directors, and employees from and against any and all injury, loss, damage, destruction or otherwise of said gem materials while in the possession of American Gemological Laboratories resulting from any cause not attributable to the negligence of American Gemological Laboratories or its employees.
The client agrees that this report is for his/her exclusive use.

Neither the American Gemological Laboratories nor any of its employees shall be responsible for any action that may be taken on the basis of this report.

This Certificate or the name of American Gemological Laboratories, Inc. may not be reproduced in whole or in part without the express, prior written authorization from American Gemological Laboratories.

Do not accept copies, alterations or corrections on this document for final transactions.

A sample AGL colored gemstone report providing identification and a
full quality evaluation, country of origin, and information pertaining to the *absence* of
any significant treatment.

AGTA GEMOLOGICAL TESTING CENTER

RUBY IDENTIFICATION REPORT

Date: SAMPLE
Report No. SAMPLE

The item described below has been examined by at least two professional staff gemologists of the AGTA Gemological Testing Center. The results of the examination are presented here subject to the limitations printed on the reverse of this report

Item Description: Loose Stone

Number of gems examined:	1
Color:	Red
Transparency:	Transparent
Weight (ct):	2.94
Dimensions (mm):	9.29 x 6.86 x 5.00
Shape:	Oval
Cut:	Mixed, Brilliant Crown
Enhancement:	None, no indications of enhancement by heat[1]

Result: **NATURAL RUBY**

Origin: **BURMA (MYANMAR)[2]**

Comments: [1]It is rare for a ruby to have not been enhanced by heat. [2]The data obtained during the examination of this stone indicates that the probable geographic origin is as stated (see below for testing techniques).

The reverse of this page is an integral part of the report, it contains important information that may help in the interpretation of the information on this side.

Garry Du Toit

Kenneth Scarratt

For and on behalf of the
AGTA GEMOLOGICAL TESTING CENTER

Tests Carried Out to Establish the Identity of the Ruby Described Herein							
Refractive index ☒	Specific gravity ☐	Hand spec ☒	Microscope ☒	Polariscope ☒	FTIR ☐	Others ☒	
Radiography ☐	Raman ☐	UV/VIS/NIR ☐	Image spec ☐	XRD ☐	EDXRF ☒		

American Gem Trade Association Gemological Testing Center, 18 East 48 th Street, Suite 1002, New York, NY 10017, USA
Tel: 212.752.1717 Fax: 212.750.0930

A sample AGTA report providing identification, country of origin, and information indicating the ruby is *not* treated

SCHWEIZERISCHES GEMMOLOGISCHES INSTITUT
INSTITUT SUISSE DE GEMMOLOGIE
SWISS GEMMOLOGICAL INSTITUTE

Falknerstrasse 9
CH-4001 **Basel** / Switzerland

Telephone   061 / 262 0640
Telefax   061 / 262 0641
Postcheck   80-15013-2

SSEF

TEST REPORT   No. 00000

on the authenticity of the following gemstone,
mounted in a brooch with diamonds

Shape & cut:	antique cushion, modified brilliant / step cut
Total weight:	approximately 27.5 grams (including mounting and diamonds)
Measurements:	approximately 24.10 x 14.05 x 12.40 mm
Calculated weight :	approximately 41 ct
Colour:	blue of medium saturation
Identification:	S A P P H I R E (variety of corundum)
Comments:	The analysed properties confirm the authenticity of this transparent sapphire. No indications of thermal enhancement.
	Origin: Kashmir

Important note: The conclusions on this Test Report reflect our findings at the time it is issued. A gemstone can be modified and / or
enhanced at any time. Therefore, the SSEF can reconfirm at any time that the stone is in accordance with the Test Report.

Please see comments on reverse side.

SSEF - SWISS GEMMOLOGICAL INSTITUTE
Gemstone Testing Division

Basel, 6 August 2001 ss

SPECIMEN

Dr. L. Kiefert, FGA   Prof. Dr. H.A. Hänni, FGA

A sample SSEF colored gemstone report providing identification,
treatment information, and country of origin

**The Gem Testing Laboratory
of Great Britain**

1242563

SAMPLE

GEM TESTING REPORT

Examined a loose, green, heart shaped, faceted stone, measuring approximately 13.50 x 14.00 x 7.50 mm. and weighing 8.30 ct.

Found to be a **NATURAL EMERALD**.

Evidence of moderate clarity enhancement present.

COMMENTS

In our opinion the country of origin of this natural emerald is **COLOMBIA**.

Most emeralds undergo clarity enhancement with colourless substances such as oils or resins since they contain surface reaching fissures.

The Gem Testing Laboratory of Great Britain is the official CIBJO recognised Laboratory for Great Britain

Only the original report with signatures and embossed stamp is a valid identification document.
This report is issued subject to the conditions printed overleaf.

The Gem Testing Laboratory of Great Britain

GAGTL, 27 Greville Street,
London, ECIN 8SU, Great Britain

Telephone: +44 171 405 3351
Fax: +44 171 831 9479

SAMPLE

Signed_____

T. Lodge FGA DGA

Signed_____

Stephen J. Kennedy FGA DGA

Date_____ 21st May 2001

A sample report from the Gem Testing Laboratory of Great Britain providing identification, treatment information, and country of origin

Hoge Raad voor Diamant vzw
Diamond High Council

GEMSTONE REPORT   N°   R0047/2001

Shape	Square	cushion	
Weight	8,005 ct		
Measurements	11,610 mm	11,330 mm	6,040 mm
Transparency	Transparent		
Colour	deep	Blue	
Identification	natural SAPPHIRE (variety of corundum)		
Comments	no indications of thermal enhancement		
	ORIGIN : Gemmological examinations revealed characteristics consistent with those of sapphires originating from KASHMIR .		

Antwerp,   05 april 2001

Gemmologist

Senior Gemmologist
Head of Laboratory

The here mentioned findings result from scientific measurements and observations carried out in the laboratory of the Diamond High Council and, when necessary, in the Physics Laboratories of the University of Antwerp (Ruca). The decisions are taken according to the knowledge and literature about gemstones known at the time of the examination.

HRD - INSTITUTE OF GEMMOLOGY   Hoveniersstraat 22 - B-2018 ANTWERPEN 1
Tel. (+32) 03 222 05 11   Fax (+32) 03 222 07 04   E-mail gem_lab@hrd.be

A sample report from HRD providing identification, information indicating that the sapphire is *not* treated, and country of origin

GÜBELIN
GEM LAB

EDELSTEIN-BERICHT · RAPPORT DE PIERRE PRECIEUSE
GEMSTONE REPORT

No.	**SPECIMEN**
Datum · Date	16 May 2001
Gegenstand · Objet · Item	One faceted gemstone
Gewicht · Poids · Weight	**3.07 ct**
Schliff · Taille · Cut	
Form · Forme · Shape	oval
Stil · Style · Style	modified brilliant cut
Abmessungen · Dimensions · Measurements	11.16 x 7.98 x 5.53 mm
Transparenz · Transparence · Transparency	transparent
Farbe · Couleur · Colour	**green**

IDENTIFIKATION · IDENTIFICATION

Spezies · Espèce · Species
NATURAL TOURMALINE

Varietät · Variété · Variety

Bemerkungen · Commentaires · Comments

GEMMOLOGISCHES LABOR · LABORATOIRE GEMMOLOGIQUE · GEMMOLOGICAL LABORATORY
Maihofstrasse 102 · CH-6000 Lucerne 9 · Switzerland · Tel. (41) 41 - 429 17 17 · Fax (41) 41 - 429 17 34
www.gubelinlab.com · e-mail: gubelinlab@compuserve.com

Christopher P. Smith, G.G.   C. Dunaigre, A.G., DUG

A Gübelin report providing identification only.
Note that "natural" tourmaline does *not* mean the stone is untreated;
natural here means it is not a synthetic or imitation.
This report does not provide treatment information, or quality
information, but more complete reports are available upon request.

CHAPTER FIVE

Colored Gemstone Synthesis & Treatment

In addition to the wide variety of natural gemstone alternatives from which to choose today, numerous synthetic and treated materials are available. They make attractive jewelry, but you must understand what you have, and pay the appropriate price for it.

All Synthetics Are Not the Same

Scientific advances and new technology have resulted in a whole world of *synthetic* gemstone materials, but it's important to understand that a synthetic is *not* an imitation. Technically, the term synthetic indicates that the material is artificially made by *using the same chemical ingredients found in natural products*—in other words, using Mother Nature's recipe. This means that a synthetic gemstone will have essentially the same physical, chemical, and optical properties observed in natural gemstones. From a practical standpoint, this also means that they will respond to various gem-identification tests in the same way as do natural stones. This can make them difficult to distinguish from the natural gem.

An *imitation* is also artificially made but not by using "nature's recipe," so it is very different physically and chemically from the gem it is imitating, and it is very easy to distinguish it from the natural gem with standard gem-identification techniques. For example, a glass "gem" is an imitation. Red glass could imitate ruby. But it resembles ruby only in *color*; a quick examination with a simple jeweler's loupe would reveal telltale signs that it is glass, and any gemological test would clearly corroborate this conclusion.

Today there are numerous synthetic gems, but they are not all produced the same way. Some are produced inexpensively, and although they are made with nature's recipe, they don't really look like the natural gem. Some are made quickly by a process very different from nature's. These are often confused with imitations because of their unnatural appearance and low cost. This type of synthetic is widely available today and has been made for almost a hundred years.

In recent years, technological advances have enabled scientists to create environments that come much closer to duplicating what is found in nature. As a result, crystals can actually be "grown" in laboratories, creating a product that very closely resembles the natural gem. These are often called flux-grown, created, or laboratory-grown synthetics. These laboratory-grown synthetics are expensive to produce and cost much more than other synthetics; in fact, the cost can be so high that consumers sometimes mistakenly conclude they are natural gemstones. Next to the natural, there is nothing that can compare to a fine lab-grown synthetic, and even though the stone may be expensive, the cost is only a fraction of that of a rare, natural gem with a comparable appearance.

Synthetics can make excellent alternatives for buyers unable to afford natural gems in the quality they desire. Be sure, however, not to confuse terms such as *created* or *grown* with *naturally created* or *grown*. All synthetic products are made by humankind. Also, remember that inexpensive synthetics are abundant, so if you are paying a premium for the stone, be sure you have a lab-grown synthetic and not an inexpensive type. As you shop around and compare various synthetic products, you will find that there are significant visual differences among them. Develop an eye for the type you want.

Gemstone Treatment Is Routine in Today's Jewelry Scene

The use of various treatments to improve the appearance of gemstones is not new. We find evidence of treatment in antique jewels, and ancient writings from Roman times and before attest to a long-standing knowledge of ways to improve the appearance of many gemstones. What is new, however, is the *routine* use of treatments, which began in the 1960s, necessitated by an ever-declining supply of natural, fine-quality gemstones. *Natural* emeralds, rubies, and sapphires—that is, gems not subjected to any type of artificial treatment or enhancement—have never been rarer than they are today. It is fair to say that if it were not for the use of various treatments, the supply of beautiful gemstones would be virtually depleted by now, and only the wealthiest and most powerful would be enjoying them!

While they can still be found, locating a natural gem in a particular size and quality can take months of intensive searching. When one is found, it can command a price prohibitive to all but the most serious collector or connoisseur. I was recently retained to help a couple acquire an exceptionally fine Colombian emerald. After discussing the options with me, and learning about different fillers and degrees of treatment used on emerald, they were willing to accept a stone with "minor traces of oil." They did not want a stone treated with other types of filler, however, or a stone with more than minimal treatment. It took several months to find the 3.64-carat emerald they selected, and the cost—at wholesale— was almost $100,000! Helping another couple search for an exceptionally fine 5-carat natural sapphire of Kashmir origin took almost as long, and the wholesale cost was over $50,000. This is not what people usually want, and most retail jewelers don't keep such gems in their regular inventory.

Most treatments simply continue the process that Mother Nature started; all gems are exposed to heat, and many to radiation, as they are forming in nature. Today, most rubies, sapphires, and many other gemstones are routinely treated with heat or exposed to some type of radiation to change or enhance their color and improve clarity, and pricing is based on the assumption that enhancement has occurred. On the other hand, if the color of a gem is very fine, and if it can be documented that the color is natural and that there is no clarity enhancement, the stone will command a much higher price. Since such gems are very rare today, some of the best sources of fine, natural-color gems are major estate pieces that sometimes reenter the market when well-known auction houses hold their "magnificent" or "important" jewelry sales.

Whether from an auction house or another source, fine rare gems with natural color and clarity normally will be accompanied by a gem-testing report verifying that fact. Without a report, or any representations to the contrary, assume that the color of any gemstone sold today has been enhanced in some manner and that the clarity may also have been improved in the process. When you are buying any expensive rare gem represented to be natural, be sure it is accompanied by a report from a respected gem-testing lab that verifies this fact, or make the purchase contingent on getting a report.

Some of the most common types of treatment include the following.

Heating

Subjecting certain gems to sophisticated heating procedures is a practice that is accepted within the jewelry industry as long as the change induced is *permanent*. Most sapphires and rubies are heated. The treatment may lighten, darken, or completely change the color and improve the clarity by melting some of the fine "silk" inclusions often present. A skilled gemologist or gem-testing laboratory can often determine whether or not the color of these gems has been altered by heating by examining the stone's *inclusions* under the microscope. Sapphire and ruby, for example, can withstand high temperatures, but often the heat causes small crystal inclusions present inside the stone to melt or explode. These altered inclusions then provide the evidence of heating.

It may be easy to determine that a stone *has* been heated, but it is often impossible to know for certain that it has *not* been—that is, that its color is natural. Making this determination can require a high degree of skill and sophisticated equipment, often only available at a major laboratory, and even then, it may not be possible to ascertain definitively. Gemologists must carefully examine the internal characteristics of the particular stone. Sometimes they see an unaltered inclusion that would lead to a conclusion that the color is natural; other times they see an altered inclusion that indicates treatment; and sometimes the inclusions, or changes and abnormalities in them, that one seeks to make a positive determination simply are not present. When there is nothing inside the gem to indicate whether it has or has not been heated, we cannot be sure.

Most rubies and sapphires sold since the 1960s have been heated to enhance their color and clarity. Other gemstones that are routinely heated today include amber, amethyst, aquamarine, pink beryl (morganite), carnelian, citrine, kunzite, tanzanite, pink topaz, several varieties of tourmaline, and zircon.

Radiation

Radiation techniques are relatively new. Frequently used on a wide range of gemstones, radiation is sometimes combined with heating. The effect is permanent on some stones, and accepted in the trade; it is not acceptable on other stones because the color fades or changes back to its original over a relatively short time. There are still some questions regarding radiation levels and the long-term effects on health. The Nuclear Regulatory Agency has been working to establish standards, and the GIA Gem Trade Laboratory now has a facility with the capability to test gemstones for "acceptable" and six "unacceptable" radiation levels.

Virtually all blue topaz sold in jewelry stores has been irradiated to obtain the various blue shades that have become so popular. Other gemstones that may have been irradiated to obtain color include deep blue beryl (called maxixe; this color will always fade); yellow beryl; diamond; kunzite; yellow or orange sapphire (not stable; will fade quickly); yellow and green topaz; and red, pink, and purple tourmaline.

Diffusion Treatment

Diffusion is a newcomer to the world of treated gemstones and is already surrounded by controversy. Diffusion (sometimes called deep diffusion or surface diffusion) is a process that alters the color of a gem by exposing the surface to certain chemicals and heating it over a prolonged period of time. At present the procedure has been used successfully to produce blue sapphire, ruby, and green topaz.

The material being treated is usually colorless or very, very pale, and *the beautiful color produced by the treatment is confined to the surface of the gem only.* If you sliced one in half, you would see an essentially colorless stone with a very narrow rim of color along its perimeter. This could create a problem if the stone is ever badly chipped or nicked and needs to be recut or polished; the surface color might be removed in the recutting, leaving a colorless stone in its place. The treatment could be repeated, should this happen, to restore the original color. When repeated on a previously diffused stone, the process requires less time, and the restored color is virtually identical to the original.

It is possible that the process will be improved to produce a treatment in which color penetrates the entire stone. At this time, however, deep diffusion simply means that the color penetrates a little deeper than in the earliest diffused stones. The color is still confined to the surface. Diffusion treatment can also produce asterism (a star effect in sapphire and ruby.)

Unfortunately many surface-diffused blue sapphires have been found mixed in with parcels of nondiffused sapphires, and some may inadvertently have been set in jewelry and sold. So it is important to buy any fine blue sapphire only from a knowledgeable, reputable jeweler. I also recommend double-checking for diffusion to avoid any unintentional misrepresentation. Ask your jeweler if he or she has the means to check for you; in many cases it is a simple, quick test with magnification and an immersion cell. If this is not possible, be sure to make the sale contingent on the stone's not being diffused, and take it to a gemologist for verification. Your jeweler or gemologist can also submit any stone in question to a major gem lab. If you should find the stone is diffused, you should have no problem exchanging it, getting a reduced price, or obtaining a refund.

Diffused stones offer beautiful choices at affordable prices. Just be sure you know whether or not the stone is diffused. If it is, pay the right price for it, and exercise some care in wearing and handling it.

At this time, diffusion treatment is being used with sapphire, with ruby, and to produce green topaz, but this treatment could have application to other gemstone materials in the future.

Fracture Filling

Fractures can interrupt light as it travels through a colored gemstone, creating a whitishness in the area of the fracture or, in some cases, reflecting back and making the fracture more noticeable. If a surface-reaching fracture is filled with the proper substance, the light will continue to pass through without blockage or reflection, so the color is not diminished and reflective fractures are much less noticeable because the reflectivity is greatly reduced. Certain gemstones, such as emerald, have more fractures than other gemstones because they form under extremely violent geological conditions. For this reason, emeralds are usually treated with fillers to reduce the visibility of fractures. The jewelry trade has always considered the oiling of emerald an acceptable practice, and it has been used routinely for many years. We don't know when the oiling of emerald began, but the practice was known during the Roman period, and we find many antique emerald pieces that still show traces of oil when examined with a microscope.

Today, gemstone treaters use various substances to fill fractures, including oil, wax, paraffin, glass, and various formulations of epoxy resin. Gemstones that may be treated with one of these substances include emerald, aquamarine, peridot, jade, turquoise, ruby, sapphire, and, in rare cases, alexandrite and garnet. Be especially alert to the possibility of fillers in ruby and sapphire; many rubies and sapphires from several new deposits contain reflective inclusions, so the use of oil and wax to improve the appearance of ruby and sapphire is increasing.

Affordable Beauty

Treated gemstones can be a way for consumers to own lovely pieces at affordable prices. The most important consideration, here as in all purchases of gemstones, is to know exactly what you are buying. While some fraudulent practices involving treated stones certainly exist (see chapter 6), selling them is perfectly legitimate so long as all the facts are disclosed, the type of treatment used for enhancement is acceptable in the trade, and all important representations are stated on the bill of sale. With these safeguards you can be reasonably secure about the purchase you are contemplating and can enjoy the fine color and beauty of a treated stone for many years to come.

A Guide to Gemstone Treatments*

Name of Gemstone	Type of Treatment Used†	Frequency	Stability	Care Required	Comments
Alexandrite	O: to reduce visibility of fractures	Rarely	Very good/fair	Normal	Usually natural
Amber	H: to add spangles and improve color	Usually	Good to very good	Special	Avoid chemicals, ultrasonic cleaners
	D: surface treated	Rarely	Variable	Special	Avoid chemicals, ultrasonic cleaners
Amethyst (see quartz)					
Ametrine (see quartz)					
Ammolite	I: to increase stability	Usually	Good to fair	Special	Avoid heat, ultrasonic cleaners, chemicals
Beryl					
Aquamarine	H: to produce purer blue	Usually	Excellent	Normal	
Blue (maxixe) deep sapphire blue)	R: to create blue from colorless or pale pink	Always	Poor	Extra special	Color fades; avoid light/heat
Emerald	O: to reduce visibilty of fractures	Usually	Very good to fair	Special	Avoid sudden temperature changes, steaming, chemicals, ultrasonic cleaners
	D: dye injected into fractures	Occasionally	Variable	Special	Same as above
Pink	H: to create purer pink	Commonly	Excellent	Normal	
Yellow-green	None	NA	NA	Normal	
Red	O	Commonly	Very good to fair	Special	Avoid ultrasonic cleaners, high heat/steam, chemicals
Yellow	R: to intensify color	Usually	Variable	Normal to special	Avoid prolonged exposure to light and heat

*Based on information developed by the American Gem Trade Association (AGTA)

† Key to symbols at end of chart

	Treatment				
Chrysoberyl					
Cat's-eye	**R**: to change color	Occasionally	Excellent	Normal	Treatment by neutron radiation can create radioactive gemstones that may be dangerous to health: test at lab
Transparent varieties					
Alexandrite (*see Alexandrite*)					
Yellow	**None**	NA	NA	Normal	
Brown	**None**	NA	NA	Normal	
Green	**None**	NA	NA	Normal	
Citrine (*see quartz*)					
Coral					
Black	**None**	NA	NA	Normal	
White	**B**	Commonly	Good	Special	Avoid chemicals, cosmetics, ultrasonic cleaners
Pink	**W**	Commonly	Good	Special	"
Orange	**I**: stabilized with plastic	Commonly	Good	Special	"
Red	**D**	Occasionally	Variable	Special to extra special depending on dye used	"
Corundum					
Ruby	**H**: to improve color and clarity	Usually	Excellent	Normal	Avoid chemicals, ultrasonic cleaners
	D: with colored oil	Occasionally	Poor	Special	
	F: with several substances including glass	Commonly	Very good to fair	Special	Fracture-filled rubies may be fragile, and filler may come out under extreme pressure: avoid heat, ultrasonic cleaners

Chart continues on next page.

Name of Gemstone	Type of Treatment Used	Frequency	Stability	Care Required	Comments
Corundum *(cont.)*					
Ruby *(cont.)*	**R**: to change color	Rarely	Unpredictable	Normal	
	U: to create color in colorless or to create star effect	Occasionally	Good	Special	Avoid repolishing, recutting since color is only on surface
Sapphire	**H**: to improve color, clarity	Usually	Excellent	Normal	
	U: to create color in colorless sapphire or to create star effect	Occasionally	Good	Special	Avoid repolishing, recutting since color is only on surface
	R: to change color	Occasionally	Very poor	Extra special	Fades quickly in heat and light
Emerald *(see beryl)*					
Garnet††					
Almandine	None	NA	NA	Normal	Avoid sudden temperature changes
Demantoid	None	NA	NA	Normal	"
Pyrope	None	NA	NA	Normal	"
Rhodolite	None	NA	NA	Normal	"
Spessartite	None	NA	NA	Normal	"
Tsavorite	None	NA	NA	Normal	"
Hematite	None	NA	NA	Normal	
Iolite	None	NA	NA	Normal	
Jade					
Jadeite	**W**: with colorless wax	Commonly	Fair	Normal to special	Avoid ultrasonic cleaners
	B followed by **W**	Rarely	Poor	Special	Avoid heat, chemicals, ultrasonic cleaners
Green/white, purple	**B** followed by **I**	Commonly	Very good to good	Special	"

		Rarely	Unknown	Special	
Nephrite	D				Avoid strong light, ultrasonic cleaners, chemicals
Kunzite (*see spodumene*)					
Lapis lazuli	W	Commonly	Fair	Normal to special	Avoid chemicals, ultrasonic cleaners
	D	Commonly	Variable	Special	"
Malachite	W	Occasionally	Fair	Special	"
	I	Rarely	Good	Special	"
Moonstone	None	NA	NA	Normal	
Opal					
White, black, semi-black	O: with oil, wax, resins	Rarely	Fair	Special	Avoid ultrasonic cleaners, heat, solvents
	I: with colorless plastic to improve durability	Rarely	Good	Special	Avoid heat, solvents
Matrix	D: by sugar-acid chemical reaction	Commonly	Good	Special (repolishing)	Avoid solvents
Boulder	O	Occasionally	Fair	Special	Avoid heat, chemicals, ultrasonic cleaners, repolishing
Fire opal	None	NA	NA	Special	Avoid heat
Peridot	O	Rarely	Good to fair	Special	Avoid sudden temperature changes, harsh chemicals, ultrasonic cleaners
Quartz					
Amethyst	H: to lighten color or remove smokiness	Often	Excellent	Special	Avoid long exposure to sunlight or heat
Ametrine	H: to create yellow part	Occasionally	Excellent	None	

Chart continues on next page.

Name of Gemstone	Type of Treatment Used	Frequency	Stability	Care Required	Comments
Quartz (*cont.*)					
Citrine	**H**: to get yellow from other quartz varieties	Usually	Excellent	Normal	
Chalcedony varieties					
Agate	D	Usually	Excellent to good	Normal	
Black onyx	D	Always	Excellent to good	Normal	
Banded	D	Usually	Excellent to good	Normal	
Blue	D	Commonly	Good to fair	Special	Some fade in light/heat
Green	D	Usually	Good to fair	Special	Some fade in light/heat
Carnelian	**H**: to produce color	Usually	Excellent	Normal	
Jasper	D: to imitate other gems	Occasionally	Excellent	Normal	
Chrysoprase	None	NA	NA	Normal	
Rhodonite	D: to even out color	Occasionally	Poor	Special	Avoid chemicals, ultrasonic cleaners
Ruby (*see corundum*)					
Sapphire (*see corundum*)					
Serpentine	**D** or **W**	Commonly	Good to fair	Special	Dye may fade; avoid ultrasonic cleaners
Sodalite	D	Rarely	Fair	Special	Dye may fade; avoid acetone
Spinel	**None**	NA	NA	Normal	
Spodumene					
Kunzite	**H**	Commonly	Fair	Special	For natural or heated, avoid strong light, ultrasonic cleaners
	R	Commonly	Fair	Special	

Green	R: to produce color	Rarely	Poor	Extra special	Color fades in light, heat
Yellow	R: to produce color	Rarely	Poor	Extra special	Color fades in light, heat
Sugilite	**None**	NA	NA	Normal	
Tanzanite	H: to produce blue/violet color	Usually	Excellent	Special	Avoid sudden temperature change; may be somewhat brittle so wear with care
Topaz					
Blue	**R** and **H**: to produce blue	Usually	Excellent	Special	Some may be radioactive; test at lab
Yellow/orange	R: to intensify color	Occasionally	Variable	Special	Avoid heat, strong light
Pink/red	H: to produce pink/red from orange and pinkish brown stones	Usually	Excellent	Normal	
Brown	**None**	NA	NA	Normal	
Green	R: to produce color	Occasionally	Poor	Extra special	Color fades in sunlight
	U: surface color only	Usually	Good	Special	Don't repolish or recut
Tourmaline					
Chrome green	**None**	NA	NA	Normal	Avoid sudden temperature changes, steaming, chemicals, ultrasonic cleaners
Yellow/orange	H: to improve color	Rarely	Good	Normal	
Green, blue	H: to improve color	Commonly	Good	Normal	
	O: to improve clarity	Occasionally	Good to fair	Special	
Pink, red, purple	H: to improve color	Occasionally	Excellent	Normal	
	R: to intensify color	Commonly	Good	Normal	
	O: to improve clarity	Occasionally	Good to fair	Special	"
	D: to improve color	Occasionally	Fair to poor	Special	"

Chart continues on next page.

Name of Gemstone	Type of Treatment Used	Frequency	Stability	Care Required	Comments
Turquoise	I: to improve color, durability	Commonly	Good	Special	Avoid hot water and household cleaners
	W: to create color	Commonly	Fair to poor	Special	"
	D: to improve color	Rarely	Poor	Extra special	"
Zircon					
Green, brown	None	NA	NA	Special	Avoid abrasives; may be brittle so wear with care
Yellow	H: to improve color	Rarely	Good	Special	"
Blue, colorless	H: to change brownish crystals to colorless and blue	Always	Fair to poor	Special	Avoid abrasives, strong light; may be brittle so wear with care
Red	H: to change brownish crystals to red	Commonly	Fair to poor	Special	"

Key to Table: **Symbols for specific types of enhancements used**

B: bleaching—using heat, light, or chemical agents to lighten or take out color from a gemstone

D: dyeing—infusing a coloring agent into a gemstone to create color, change color, enrich color, or produce the appearance of more even color distribution

F: filling—filling surface-reaching fractures or cavities with *colorless* glass, plastic, solidified borax, or similar substances, which are visible to a trained gemologist using 10x magnification with proper lighting

H: heating—the use of heat to alter or improve color and clarity, and to create optical phenomena such as a cat's-eye or star effect

I: impregnation—using a *colorless* substance, usually plastic, to impregnate a porous gemstone to improve appearance and/or durability

O: oiling/resin infusion—using *colorless* oil, wax, resin, or other substances, except glass or plastic, to fill surface-reaching fractures to improve appearance

R: irradiation—using neutron, gamma and/or electron bombardment to alter a gemstone's color; irradiation treatment may be combined with heating

U: diffusion—coating the surface of a gemstone with chemicals and heating at high temperatures to produce color on the surface of a gemstone, or to produce a star effect

W: waxing/oiling—impregnating a porous opaque gemstone such as turquoise or a translucent gemstone such as jade with *colorless* wax, paraffin, or oil to improve appearance

††The use of fillers in garnet to reduce visibility of fractures has been reported in several extremely rare cases; typically garnet is not enhanced.

CHAPTER SIX

Fraud & Misrepresentation in Colored Gems

I would like to begin by emphasizing here that the percentage of misrepresentation and fraud among total jewelry transactions is quite low, and that most jewelers are reputable professionals in whom you can place your trust. In the colored-gem market, there is a greater occurrence of misrepresentation than in the diamond market, however, primarily because of the scientifically complex nature of colored stones. So it is even more important to be aware of the deceptive practices you might encounter when buying a colored gem, both to protect yourself from the more obvious scams and to better understand the importance of dealing with a reliable jeweler. I also stress the importance, to an even greater degree, of seeking verification from a qualified gemologist—one with extensive experience with colored gems—when buying any expensive colored gem to ensure that your gemstone is what it is represented to be.

Misrepresenting Synthetic as Natural

Today it is very important to verify the genuineness of any fine, valuable gemstone because the new generation of synthetic products is so similar to the natural that the two can be easily confused. As I discussed in chapter 5, many very fine synthetics are available, and they can make attractive jewelry choices when properly represented. Still, you should protect yourself from intentional and sometimes unintentional misrepresentation.

Synthetics have been on the market for many years. Good synthetic sapphires, rubies, and spinels have been manufactured commercially since the early 1900s, and very good synthetic emeralds since the 1940s. While these early synthetics were attractive and popular because of their very low price, they didn't really look like natural stones. Most looked "too good to be true," so that they were readily distinguished from the real thing by a competent jeweler.

Today, this is often not the case. While older techniques for producing synthetics are still used and their products are still easy to recognize, new, sophisticated methods result in products that no longer possess the signature characteristics with which gem dealers and jewelers have long been familiar. To further complicate matters of identification, synthetics now often contain characteristics very similar to their natural counterparts. As a result, some are being sold as natural, intentionally and unintentionally. A gemologist with extensive experience, or a gem-testing laboratory such as GIA or AGL, can differentiate between them and verify genuineness.

A true experience dramatically illustrates why making the extra effort required to verify genuineness is so important. I know a jeweler with an excellent reputation for honesty, reliability, and professional expertise. He had been in the business for many years and had extensive gemological training. Nonetheless, he bought a new type of synthetic ruby as a natural stone, then sold it to a customer for just under $10,000.

His customer, who had purchased the stone at a reasonable price, proceeded to resell it to a third party for a quick profit. The third party took it to a very competent gemologist with a reputation for having the skill and equipment necessary to identify new synthetic materials. The truth about the stone quickly came to light. The second and third parties in this case lost nothing (one of the benefits of buying from a reputable jeweler). The jeweler, however, suffered both a heavy financial loss and considerable damage to his reputation.

You may ask how he made such a mistake. It was easy. He was knowledgeable, like many other jewelers, and thought he knew how to distinguish a natural from a synthetic stone. But he had not kept current on technological advances and new synthetic products entering the marketplace. So he made an over-the-counter purchase of this lovely stone from a private party who had procured it in Asia. Many of these new synthetics are produced in the United States and then find their way to Asia—the source of many natural stones—where they are more easily sold as the "real thing." The jeweler had no recourse because he had no way of locating the seller, who had simply walked in off the street.

As this story shows, it is essential to have a highly qualified gemologist verify authenticity, particularly for fine rubies, emeralds, and sapphires. Thousands of dollars may be at stake, for jewelers may innocently buy one of these stones, believing it to be natural, and pass their error on to the customer. Don't delude yourself into believing that if a piece is purchased from a well-respected firm it is always what it is represented to be; even the best-known firms have made mistakes in this area. It may be inconvenient to obtain an expert analysis, and it may require an additional expense, but I believe it is better to be safe now than sorry later.

With sophisticated modern equipment and a greater knowledge of crystals, humans can now "create" or "grow" almost any gemstone. As a general rule, remember that any gem—amethyst, alexandrite, ruby, emerald, sapphire, opal, or even turquoise—could be synthetic, that many synthetics are themselves expensive, and that most have become more difficult to distinguish from their natural counterparts, resulting in inadvertent misrepresentation. So make sure you take time to verify a stone's true identity.

Simulated Stones

As already discussed (see chapter 5), simulated or imitation stones should not be confused with synthetics, which possess essentially the same physical, chemical, and optical properties of the natural gem. A simulated stone is usually a very inexpensive artificial imitation that resembles the natural stone in color, but little else. Many imitations are glass, but they can also be plastic. Imitations, or simulants as they are also called, are very easily differentiated from the genuine by careful visual examination and simple gemological testing. There are glass simulations of all the colored stones, and glass and plastic simulated pearls, turquoise, and amber are also common.

Imitations are frequently found in estate jewelry, sometimes mixed with natural gems in the same piece.

Look-Alike Substitution

Another form of deception involves misrepresenting a more common, less expensive stone for a rarer, more expensive gem of similar color. Today, as more and more natural gemstones in a wide variety of colors enter the market, both deliberate and accidental misrepresentation can occur.

Color Alteration

As I discussed in chapter 5, color enhancement of gemstones is not new, and many techniques used routinely today have been used for generations and do not in themselves constitute fraud. Some treatments, however, should not be applied to certain gems, normally because the results are not permanent and the color may revert to the original. Such treatments are not accepted by the trade.

Because color enhancement is so common, it's important for you to understand exactly which procedures are acceptable in the industry and which represent deceptive or fraudulent practices aimed at passing off inferior stones as much more expensive ones.

Here I will discuss various treatments and explain which are routine and which may constitute fraud or misrepresentation.

Heat-Treated Stones

Subjecting stones to sophisticated heating procedures is the most commonly used method of changing or enhancing a gem's color and is used routinely on a variety of gems to lighten, darken, or completely change color. Heat treatment is not a fraudulent practice when used on certain gems, on which the results are *permanent*. **This procedure is an accepted practice routinely applied to the following stones:**

- *Amber*—to deepen color and add "sun spangles"
- *Amethyst*—to lighten color; to change color of pale material to "yellow" stones sold as citrine
- *Aquamarine*—to deepen color and remove any greenish undertone to produce a "bluer" blue
- *Carnelian*—to produce color
- *Citrine*—often produced by heating other varieties of quartz
- *Kunzite*—to improve color
- *Morganite*—to change color from orange to pinkish
- *Sapphire*—to lighten or intensify color; to improve uniformity
- *Tanzanite*—to produce a more desirable blue shade
- *Topaz*—in combination with radiation, to produce shades of blue; to produce pink
- *Tourmaline*—to lighten the darker shades, usually of the green and blue varieties
- *Zircon*—to produce red, blue, or colorless stones

The color obtained by these heating procedures is usually permanent.

Radiated Stones

Radiation techniques are now in common use, produced by any of several methods, each of which has a specific application. Sometimes radiation is used in combination with heat treatment. As long as the technique produces stable results, color enhancement by radiation techniques is not considered fraudulent.

Radiation techniques are routinely used for the following stones and do not constitute fraud:

- *Diamond*—to change the color from an off-white color to a fancy color (green, yellow, etc.)
- *Kunzite*—to darken color
- *Pearl*—to produce blue and shades of gray ("black" pearls)
- *Topaz*—to change from colorless or nearly colorless to blue; to intensify yellow and orange shades and create green
- *Tourmaline*—to intensify pink, red, and purple shades
- *Yellow beryl*—to create yellow color

Some very deep blue topazes have been found to be radioactive and may be harmful to the wearer. Most blue topaz sold in the United States since 1992 has been tested for radiation level by the GIA or other centers established for that purpose. Exercise caution when purchasing deep blue topaz outside the United States, in countries where radiation testing is not required.

As far as we know now, the color changes resulting from radiation treatment on the above stones are usually permanent. Some stones subjected to radiation, however, obtain a beautiful color that is temporary. Some irradiated "blue," "orange," and "yellow" sapphire will fade quickly. I have seen nice "yellow" sapphires treated by radiation quickly lose their color when exposed to the flame of a cigarette lighter. If you are considering a "yellow," it may be worthwhile to try this simple flame test if the jeweler will permit. If not, be sure to have it fade tested by a qualified gemologist or gem lab. Deep blue beryl known as *maxixe* beryl is created by irradiating off-color or pale beryl, but the color is *not* permanent and the color *fades quickly*. Irradiation of sapphire and blue beryl is not accepted in the trade.

When diamonds are irradiated to produce fancy colors, labs can usually determine that they have been treated. However, for most other gems on which radiation is used, testing procedures for determining whether or not color is natural have not been developed as of this date.

Diffusion-Treated Stones

Sapphire and ruby. Diffusion treatment involves introducing chemicals (the same coloring agents present in natural blue sapphire and ruby) into the surface of a colorless or nearly colorless stone, and heating the stone over a prolonged period. This treatment produces a lovely color, but on the surface of the stone only; the center remains colorless.

Diffused sapphires are being substituted for nondiffused sapphires by unscrupulous merchants and purchased by dealers and jewelers unknowingly in parcels of stones that are subsequently mounted in jewelry. They are also being set in antique and estate jewelry. When you are buying any fine sapphire today, it is important to purchase from a knowledgeable, reputable jeweler. Be especially wary of bargains! Diffusion-treated ruby is less common but warrants the same caution.

Green topaz. Diffusion treatment creates a lovely green color not found in nature.

There is nothing wrong with buying diffused stones as long as you know it and pay the right price.

Dyed Stones

Gemstones have been dyed since earliest times. Numerous examples of dyed chalcedony (an inexpensive variety of quartz) can be found in antique jewelry, imitating other gems. Gems that are frequently dyed include jade, opal, coral, lapis, and to a lesser degree poor-quality star rubies, star sapphires, and emeralds.

Dyed material may be very stable, but it can also be very temporary. We've seen dyed lapis in which the "blue" came off with a cotton ball moistened in fingernail polish remover. Dyed gems may be genuine stones that have been dyed to enhance their color (as in dyeing pale green jadeite to a deeper green), or they may be a different gem altogether.

Dyed gems should always cost less than gems with natural color. Fine lapis and jadeite should always be checked for dyeing. Here are some gemstones that are often *faked* using dyeing techniques:

- *Black onyx*—dyed chalcedony (onyx rarely occurs naturally)
- *Banded agate*—dyed chalcedony, with white bands alternating with strong-colored bands

- *Carnelian*—chalcedony dyed reddish brown
- *Chrysoprase*—chalcedony dyed green
- *Jade (jadeite)*—chalcedony dyed green to imitate fine jadeite
- *Swiss lapis*—jasper dyed blue and sold as "lapis" or "Swiss lapis"

Here are some gemstones that are often dyed to change or improve color:

- *Jade (jadeite)*—color frequently improved by dyeing to a beautiful emerald or young grass green color, to look like "imperial" jade (while jade occurs naturally in almost every color, it may also be dyed other colors)
- *Coral and lapis*—dyed to deepen the color, or create more uniform color

Blackening Techniques

These are used to alter color, not by dyeing but by introducing a chemical reaction (sugar-acid chemical reaction) that creates black carbon, which blackens the color. The following stones are commonly faked by using this treatment:

- *Black opal*—blackened white opal (black opal is more valuable and precious)
- *Black onyx*—blackened chalcedony (most of the "black onyx" sold today in jewelry is actually chalcedony)

Waxing

This is a process consisting of rubbing the stone with a tinted waxlike substance to hide surface cracks and blemishes and to slightly improve the color. It is used often on cheaper Indian star rubies and sometimes on star sapphires.

Oiling

This technique is commonly used on emeralds. The emerald is soaked in oil (which may or may not be tinted green). Its purpose is to fill fine cracks, which are fairly common in emerald. These cracks look whitish and therefore weaken the green body color of the emerald. The oil fills the cracks, making them "disappear," and thereby improves the color by eliminating the white. It can also reduce the reflectivity of cracks.

This is an accepted procedure and will normally last for many years. However, if the stone is put in a hot ultrasonic cleaner (which is dangerous to any emerald and is *never* recommended), or soaked in an organic solvent such as gasoline, xylene, or substances containing these, such as paint remover, the oil may be slowly dissolved out of the cracks and the whitish blemishes will then reappear, weakening the color. If this should happen, the stone can be re-oiled. Using green-tinted oil, however, is not an accepted trade practice.

Oiling is now used on many other gems, including sapphire and ruby.

Painting

This technique is often used with cabochon (nonfaceted) transparent ("jelly") or semitransparent opals to create a stone that looks like precious black opal. This is done by putting the stone in a closed-back setting that has a high rim (bezel). A black cement or paint is spread on the inside of the setting so that when the opal is placed inside, the light entering it gets trapped and reflected back, giving the opal the appearance of a fine black opal. (See also the section below, describing composite stones and opal doublets.)

Foil-Backed Stones

This technique is not frequently encountered in modern jewelry but is relatively common in antique jewelry, and anyone interested in antique jewelry should be aware of it. It is seen with both nonfaceted and faceted stones, set usually in a closed-back mounting. This technique involves lining the inside of the setting with silver or gold foil to add brilliance and sparkle (as with foil-backed glass imitating diamond), or with colored foil to change or enhance color by projecting color into the stone. Always be apprehensive when considering a piece of jewelry that has a closed back.

I recently examined a heavy, yellow gold cross set with five fine, flawless emeralds, which appeared to have exceptionally fine green body color. The stones were set "in the gold" so that the backs of the stones couldn't be seen. My suspicion was aroused, since the emeralds were all flawless and the color was so uniformly fine. Upon closer examination it became clear that the green body color was projected into the stones by a fine emerald green foil back. The stones were probably not even emerald, but near-colorless aquamarines. Since both aquamarine and emerald belong to the same mineral family, beryl (*emerald* is the name given to the rare green variety of beryl, while we call the more common blue variety aquamarine), an inexperienced jeweler or gemologist using standard, basic procedures to identify the stones could have erroneously identified them as fine emeralds.

Smoking

This is a technique used only on opals. It is used to give off-white to tan-colored opals from Mexico a more desirable, moderately dark coffee brown color that greatly enhances the opal fire. It consists of taking a cut and polished opal, wrapping it tightly in brown paper, and putting it in a covered container over moderate heat until the paper is completely charred. When cooled and removed, the opal now has a much more intense brown body color and fire. But if this smoke-produced color coating were to be badly scratched, the underlying color would show through and the stone would have to be resmoked.

This treatment can be easily detected by wetting the stone (preferably with saliva). While it is wet, some of the fire disappears; then it reappears after the surface has dried.

Fracture Filling with Glass and Epoxy Resins

Fractures that break the surface of a colored gem can be filled with a liquid glass or glasslike substance, or with an epoxy resin-type filler. Fillers make cracks less visible and improve a stone's overall appearance. A coloring agent can also be added to the filler to simultaneously improve a stone's overall color. Selling a filled gem without disclosure is not an accepted trade practice. To do so knowingly constitutes fraud. Nonetheless, the number of glass-filled rubies encountered in the marketplace and being sold without disclosure has increased dramatically, and emeralds filled with epoxy resin are now in wide circulation and often sold without disclosure of the presence of epoxy resin.

Composite Stones

Composite stones are exactly what the term implies: stones composed of more than one part. Composites come in two basic types. Doublets are composite stones consisting of two parts, sometimes held together by a colored bonding agent. Triplets are composite stones consisting of three parts, usually glued together to a colored middle part.

Doublets

Doublets are especially important to know about because, while they were widely used in antique jewelry before the development of synthetics, today they are making a comeback and reappearing throughout the jewelry market.

In antique pieces, the most commonly encountered doublet, often referred to as a *false doublet,* consists of a red garnet top fused to an appropriately colored glass bottom. With the right combination, any colored gem could be simulated by this method. Garnets were used for the top portion of these false doublets because they possessed nice luster and excellent durability and were readily available in great quantity, which made them very inexpensive.

Another form of the doublet is made from two parts of a colorless material, fused together with an appropriately colored bonding agent. An "emerald" (sometimes sold as *soudé* emerald) can be made, for example, using a colorless synthetic spinel top and bottom, held together in the middle (at the girdle) by green glue. Red glue or blue glue could be used to simulate ruby or sapphire.

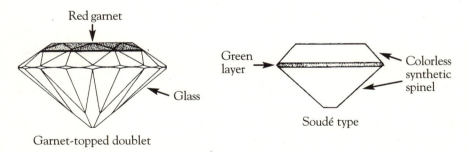

Garnet-topped doublet

Soudé type

When some composite stones are immersed in liquid (such as alcohol or methylene iodide), one can often see two or three distinct parts. With soudé emeralds, the top and bottom may seem to disappear, leaving only a green plane visible across the girdle area. (*Note:* Immersion will not reveal garnet-topped doublets.)

Colored Gemstones
The Rarest of Them All...

*Each a thing of beauty and preciousness,
unique and mysterious*

Red and Pink Gemstones to Warm Any Heart

Red gems occur in a wide range of hues and tones to please every taste and budget.

Rubellite
(Red Tourmaline)

Morganite

Kunzite

Tourmaline

Rhodolite Garnet

Topaz

Topaz

Ruby

Sapphire

Morganite

Red Beryl
(Red "Emerald")

Spinel

Rare red beryl, also referred to as red "emerald"—

Left: The crystal as it occurs in nature

Right: A brilliantly cut and polished gem waiting to be set

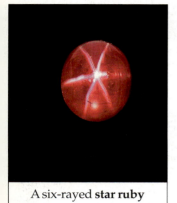

A six-rayed **star ruby**

Right:
Rhodochrosite,
an oval cabochon and a rare round faceted stone

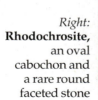

Blue Gemstones Offer Heavenly Choices

More blue stones are available today than ever before, and new discoveries—such as the exciting "neon" *Paraiba* tourmaline in the late 1980s—continue to add to the list of possibilities.

Aquamarine

Zircon

Indicolite Tourmaline

Sapphire

Blue Topaz

Tanzanite

Iolite

Translucent chrysocolla, increasingly popular for jewelry, is seen here in one of the new "fantasy" cuts.

"Neon" tourmaline from Paraiba, Brazil

Exceptionally fine **star sapphire,** showing strong star, can be very costly today.

Moonstones, exhibiting their magical "adularescence"—a bright, billowing, milky sheen moving within the stone

Yellow and Orange Gems to Brighten the Day

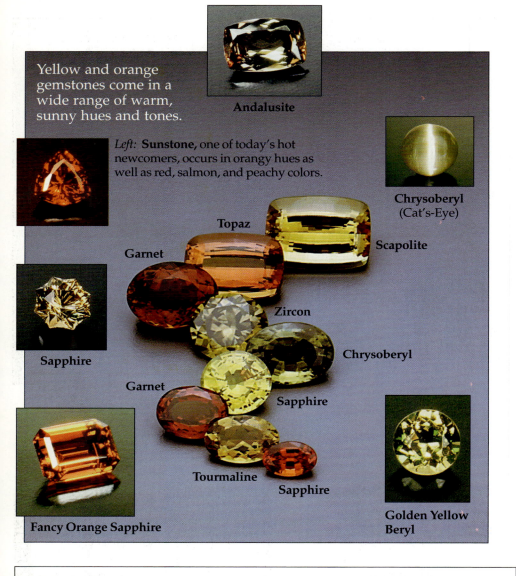

Yellow and orange gemstones come in a wide range of warm, sunny hues and tones.

Andalusite

Left: **Sunstone,** one of today's hot newcomers, occurs in orangy hues as well as red, salmon, and peachy colors.

Chrysoberyl (Cat's-Eye)

Topaz

Scapolite

Garnet

Zircon

Sapphire

Chrysoberyl

Garnet

Sapphire

Tourmaline

Sapphire

Golden Yellow Beryl

Fancy Orange Sapphire

Precious topaz, also known as "imperial" topaz

Notice the similarity in color between some citrine and topaz. Citrine is often mistaken and misrepresented as topaz. Citrine is a lovely gem, but it is less brilliant, less rare, and less costly than topaz.

Citrine, a member of the quartz family, comes in shades from pale yellow to rich amber.

Green Gems That Everyone Will Envy

Tsavorite Garnet

If green is your color, choices abound from pastel yellow-green to rich grass green.

Tourmaline

Peridot

Tourmaline

Emerald

Sapphire

Chrome Tourmaline

Tanzanite

Demantoid Garnet

Zircon

Emerald, cut in the shape that bears its name—the "emerald cut"

Paraiba Tourmaline

Fine Art Deco period brooch with very fine green **jadeite** centerpiece

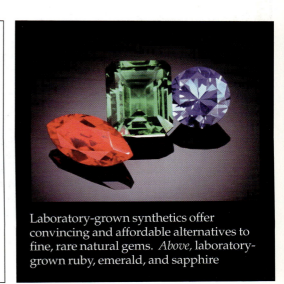

Laboratory-grown synthetics offer convincing and affordable alternatives to fine, rare natural gems. *Above,* laboratory-grown ruby, emerald, and sapphire

Opals—A Fiery World of Color

In addition to the widely available white opal, very affordable "fire" opals and rare, costly black opals create excitement.

Above: **Australian Andamooka crystal opal** and **Andamooka matrix opal** beads

Right: **Mexican "fire" opals**

Below left: **Boulder opal**
Below center: **Fine black opal**
Below right: **Boulder opal**

Classic Shapes and Cutting Styles

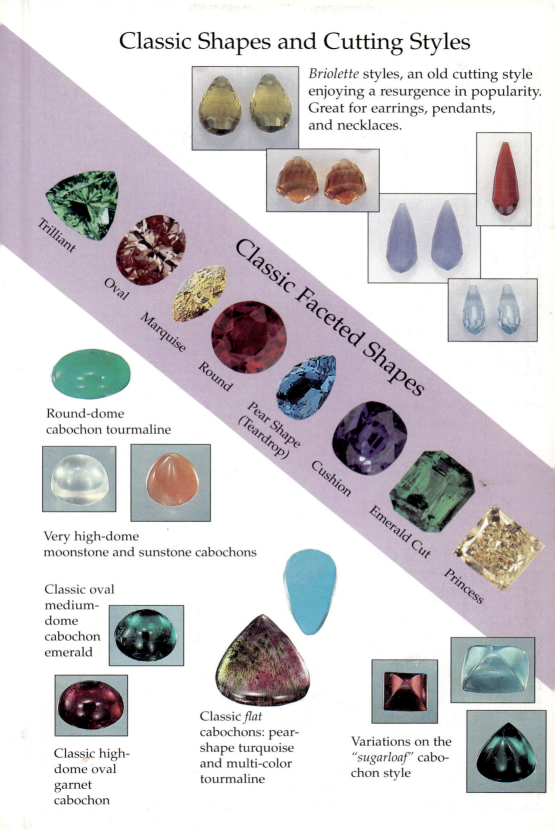

Briolette styles, an old cutting style enjoying a resurgence in popularity. Great for earrings, pendants, and necklaces.

Classic Faceted Shapes

Trilliant

Oval

Marquise

Round

Pear Shape (Teardrop)

Cushion

Emerald Cut

Princess

Round-dome cabochon tourmaline

Very high-dome moonstone and sunstone cabochons

Classic oval medium-dome cabochon emerald

Classic high-dome oval garnet cabochon

Classic *flat* cabochons: pear-shape turquoise and multi-color tourmaline

Variations on the *"sugarloaf"* cabochon style

Gemstone Cutters and Carvers…

Master cutters such as David Brackna, Michael Dyber, Mark Gronlund, Richard Homer, Glenn Lehrer, and Steve Walters are changing the world of gemstone faceting. Their innovative *concave* faceting styles—often combined with other techniques—are winning prestigious international awards and producing dramatic new looks applauded by top designers seeking unique gemstones for their distinctive creations.

PHOTOS: ROBERT WELDON

PHOTO: JOEL AREM

PHOTO: ROBERT WELDON

Triangular amethysts show effect of concave faceting (left) compared to traditional faceting.

Faceting artist David Brackna's work reflects great versatility combining concave faceting, traditional faceting, carving, and inlay.

PHOTO: ROBERT WELDON

PHOTO: ROBERT WELDON

Brackna's Optical Inlay achieves an amazing effect here; opal is inlaid above the culet of this concave faceted green beryl.

Richard Homer's suite of concave faceted gemstones attests to his skill as one of today's top award-winning artists in the world of faceting.

…Artists Creating a New Style

Artist Michael Dyber's signature Luminaire *(left)* and the Dyber Optic Dish *(below Luminaire)*. The 95-carat yellow citrine Luminaire is part of the Permanent Collection at the Carnegie Museum of Natural History, Pittsburgh, Pennsylvania.

PHOTOS: SENA DYBER

PHOTO: ROBERT WELDON

TorusRing™ gem cut created by Glenn Lehrer has the designer world in a whirl.

Master carver Steve Walters combines shape, textured black onyx, rutillated quartz, and color for striking creations that can be used in a wide range of jewelry creations.

Artist Mark Gronlund's concave faceted gem adds drama to Gary Dulac's orange citrine pendant. His 45-carat aquamarine was an *AGTA Cutting Edge Award Winner.*

PHOTOS: JOHN PARRISH

Gemstone Artists Create Objets d'Art…

From artistically executed sculptures to exquisite treasure chests to sensual "objets" to adorn the vanity, gemstone artists are moving from the jewelry salon to museums and art galleries.

One of Nicolai Medvedev's intricately executed *intarsia* boxes. Medvedev's work has been compared to that of Fabergé. His creations were on exhibition at the Smithsonian Institution in Washington, D.C.— the first one-man show ever produced for a living artist— and ran for an unprecedented 2½ years.

Michael Dyber's rich, sensual sculpture in very fine lapis

Two exquisite carvings by Glenn Lehrer. The one above is carved from lavender drusy agate, topped with a lavender pearl and diamond. The masterpiece at right is constructed like a puzzle, without metal or glue. The yellow Sapphire TorusRing™ is *friction-set* in black jade with blue chalcedony and stained-black drusy agate. It is all locked into place by a very thin, straw-like jade tube—fibrous and thin, flexible and durable. It is 3½" x 2¼".

One of David Brackna's Lightscape Optical Mosaics. The work was created from 32 pieces of amethyst, citrine, rock crystal, and ametrine and weighs 495 carats.

...and Art to Wear

Award-winning gemstone artists Susan Allen and Michael Christy have combined their unique skills to create an unparalleled collection of *essence bottles* to adorn the vanity...or travel with you as the jewels you wear! Ms. Allen does the internal carvings for Mr. Christy's romantic creations.

Susan Allen's "Ocean Magic," carved in natural quartz crystals showing three dolphins, a smiling moray eel, and "brain coral" in this whimsical three-dimensional work.

"Frog": mint green beryl, on a jade base and topped by tourmaline with rubellite "dipper"

Both of these three-dimensional works contain "dippers" that convert to pendant necklaces, and accent stones that can be removed and worn as earrings.

"Ambrosia": amethyst on a jadeite base, topped by pearl; lower base is charoite. The dipper is a natural emerald crystal, and is attached to the pearl for a stunning pendant. All accent stones are emerald, and the rubellite earrings are a surprise, hidden under the amethyst bottle. This work was on exhibition at the Carnegie Museum of Natural History, Pittsburgh, Pennsylvania.

Colorful Creations
from Winning Designers...

Above: Scott Keating's colorful use of *turret,* or *bar,* cuts.

Innovative design is focus of sundial, and innovative cutting is focus of ring in these creations by John David Cooney.

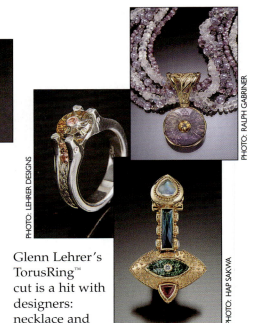

PHOTO: LEHRER DESIGNS

PHOTO: RALPH GABRINER

PHOTO: HAP SAKWA

Glenn Lehrer's TorusRing™ cut is a hit with designers: necklace and pendant by Conni Mainne *(top)*; ring by Glenn Lehrer *(center)*; pendant/brooch by Kent Raible *(bottom)*.

Designers Blend Old and New in Upcoming Collections

PHOTOS: AARON CHENEY

Designer Karl Benz puts the focus on the new square *Context*® cut, round *Spirit Sun*® cut, and the latest *marquise* cut, creating a simple but distinctive contemporary feel *(above)*. Texture, color, and movement combine to create unique brooch by Richard Kimball *(below)*.

Classic elegance is created in this necklace by Brian Sholdt, while use of the innovative *bar cut* produces a strikingly bold look in his ring and earrings.

Colored gemstones are more popular today than ever before. Unique cutting styles and unusual colors and color combinations provide top designers with limitless possibilities to create distinctive jewelry, from the traditional to the avant-garde.

Innovative use of color and bold design are the focus of this unique brooch by Ruud Kahle.

Checkerboard cut in convertible pendant/ring design creates a distinctive award-winner by Virginia Andersen.

Award-winning necklace combines classic with contemporary design by Karen Feldman

Cabochons are enjoying renewed popularity, as seen in H. Stern's Moonface collection *(right)*, and rings from Gumuchian Fils, Ltd. *(left)*.

Striking combination of cabochon with faceted stones in ring by William Richey *(left)*

James Breski offers a range of classic styles: A variety of bracelets in numerous color possibilities *(above)*; classic emerald and diamond earrings *(above right)*; and invisibly-set pendant and earrings—a technique requiring intensive labor and skill *(left)*.

Colorful Ring Designs…

Classic Designs for the Emerald Cut, Each Creating a Distinctive Look

Princess Takes Center Stage

New princess cuts in bold contemporary two-tiered geometric design.

Clockwise from top left: Emerald-cut ruby flanked on each side by two parallel straight-baguette diamonds; emerald-cut ruby with *trapezoid* diamond and *trapezoid* ruby on each side; classic emerald cut with triangular diamonds; emerald-cut ruby with two princess-cut diamonds and trilliant-cut rubies on each side; a classic square emerald-cut emerald with unusual *bullet*-shape diamonds.

Modern "Heirloom" Designs Create Nostalgic and Timeless Feeling

Elegant, classic settings create rich frame for important gemstones in these rings by designer Henry Dunay.

Meticulous detail captures heirloom feeling in this modern diamond and sapphire ring by Brian Sholdt.

Variations on the Classic Oval

Classic softness created by using pear-shape diamonds with oval.

Elegant effect created by *half-moon* cut diamonds with oval.

Straight baguette and tapered baguette define and lead eye toward the center.

Classic yet contemporary feeling created by using three tapered baguettes scrolled across the ring shoulder.

Two distinctively different rings highlight a cushion-cut center stone.
Left: A classic cushion-cut sapphire accentuated by modern trilliant-cut diamonds
Right: A cushion-cut emerald in an elegant diamond baguette frame

Classic Colored Stone Bands... Infinite Possibilities

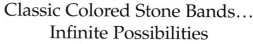

Ornamental Stones

Numerous colorful opaque and translucent materials are available for a variety of jewelry and ornamental uses, from beads to belt buckles.

Sterling belt buckles using rhodochrosite and small lapis triangles *(left)*, and lapis with small round green chrysoprase accents *(right)*, by designer Elizabeth Rand.

True doublets are created by using two genuine stone parts and fusing them together with an appropriately colored glue to create a "larger" gem of better color than the original components. For example, we sometimes see emerald doublets composed of two parts of genuine pale green emerald, fused with deep green glue to create a large, deep green "gem" emerald.

A clever version of a true doublet that we sometimes still encounter is a "sapphire" doublet composed of two pieces of genuine sapphire, but pale yellow sapphire fused together with blue glue. This creates an especially convincing "fine blue sapphire." The same techniques are used to make ruby doublets, although they don't look as convincing. And the same basic procedures can produce emerald doublets, using beryl instead of sapphire.

Opal doublets also occur, usually consisting of a thin top layer of genuine opal cemented to a base that can be either a poorer grade of opal or some other substance altogether. The most commonly encountered opal doublets are those made to look like the precious black opal. This doublet is usually composed of a translucent or transparent top, cemented by black cement to a bottom portion of cheaper opal or other material that acts as a support. Please note that the tops of these "black opal" doublets are usually not genuine black opal, though they certainly look like it.

Opal doublets are also made by cementing a thin piece of fine opal to a larger piece of less fine opal to create a larger overall appearance. The doublets can be identified by observing the *join* of the two pieces at the girdle; you can see the dark line of the cement between the two pieces.

Because so many doublets are flooding the market, those who love sapphire, ruby, and emerald must be particularly careful and buy only from reputable jewelers. I know a woman who paid $16,000 recently for a pair of "genuine" emerald earrings from a jeweler on New York's 47th Street. They contained four soudé emerald doublets and were worth only a couple of hundred dollars—and that for the gold and diamonds in the settings. Luckily, this woman had all the right information on the bill of sale, discovered the error in time, and was able to return the pieces and get her money back from the jeweler.

It is alarming to see the large number of ruby and sapphire doublets consisting of genuine tops—usually nearly colorless or a very inexpensive greenish brown color—and synthetic sapphire and ruby bottoms that are being sold as genuine. Avoid "bargains" from any merchant unless you can check them out. Be especially wary of street peddlers when you are traveling in Asia and South America. We've seen an incredible number of doublets in jewelry and "unmounted" stones brought back by unsuspecting travelers, especially those journeying to exotic spots known for gems.

Many of the doublets now appearing in jewelry sold by reputable firms were originally slipped in with genuine stones shipped to buyers around the world. Since doublets are difficult to spot and will even pass four gemological tests providing positive identification, it is easy for one to be passed on to a customer unknowingly, especially when it is set in a sleek, modern bezel setting.

There is nothing wrong with buying a doublet as long as you know what you are buying, and pay a fair price. Just be careful not to buy a doublet unknowingly. Be sure to verify all the facts.

Triplets

Triplets are frequently encountered in the opal market and have substantially replaced the doublet there. The triplet is exactly like the opal doublet except that it has a cabochon-shaped colorless quartz cap (the third part) that covers the entire doublet, giving the delicate doublet greater protection from breakage and providing greater luminescence (brightness) to the stone.

With careful examination, a competent jeweler or gemologist should be able to easily differentiate a doublet or triplet from a natural. I should note, however, that detection of an opal doublet may be very difficult if it is set in a mounting with a rim (bezel set) covering the seam where the two pieces are cemented together. It might be necessary to remove the stone from its setting for positive identification. Because of opal's fragile nature, removal must be performed only by a very competent bench jeweler (a jeweler who actually makes or repairs jewelry), and the jeweler may agree to do so only at your risk, not wanting to assume responsibility for any breakage. In the case of a black opal worth several thousand dollars, it is well worth the additional cost and inconvenience to be sure it is not a doublet worth only a few hundred dollars. Always be apprehensive when buying a "flat-topped opal" that is bezel-set.

Misleading Names

Another form of misrepresentation occurs when colored stones are called by names that lead the buyer to believe they are something they are not. This practice frequently occurs, especially outside the United States. When any stone is described with a qualifier, as in "Rio topaz," be sure to ask whether the stone is a genuine, natural stone. Ask why there is a qualifier.

Let's examine two examples: "Japanese amethyst" and "Ceylon sapphire." In the case of Japanese amethyst, the stone is not genuine but synthetic, and the name, therefore, is clearly misleading. However, in the case of the Ceylon sapphire, *Ceylon* refers to the location from which that gem was mined, and most Ceylon sapphires are always a particular tone of blue (a lighter shade, and very lively). Their color makes them much more desirable than certain other varieties, such as Australian or Thai, which are often overly dark and less brilliant. Therefore, in this case, *Ceylon* is very important to the stone's complete description.

Let's look at one more example, Ceylon-*colored* sapphire. In this case, the qualifier is the word *colored*. A Ceylon-colored sapphire is not a Ceylon sapphire but a sapphire that has a color that resembles the color of a Ceylon sapphire. In most cases, although there are rare exceptions, this qualifier also implies some type of color alteration or treatment.

There is nothing actually wrong with selling "Japanese amethyst" or "Ceylon-colored sapphire" or other similarly named stones, as long as you are told what it really is and pay the right price. Then the decision is yours: either you like it or you don't; it meets your emotional need for an amethyst or Ceylon sapphire or it doesn't; and the price is right or it isn't. The following tables provide some examples of names to be aware of: "descriptive" names that are important to the stone's complete description; and misnomers—misleading names that are meant to do exactly that, mislead.

Descriptive Names	Misnomers (And What They Really Are)

Emerald

African emerald (emerald mined in Africa)	*Chatham emerald* (synthetic)
Brazilian emerald (emerald mined in Brazil)	*Esmeralda emerald* (green tourmaline)
	Evening emerald (peridot)
	Lannyte emerald (doublet)
Colombian emerald (emerald mined in Colombia; the best quality is considered by connoisseurs to be the finest; rare and very expensive)	*Mascot emerald* (doublet)
	Oriental emerald (green sapphire)
	Soudé emerald (doublet)
Indian emerald (emerald mined in India)	
Pakistan emerald (emerald mined in Pakistan)	
Zambian emerald (emerald mined in Zambia)	

Jade

Ax stone (nephrite jade)	*African jade* (green massive garnet)
California jade (both jadeite and nephrite jade)	*Australian jade* (chrysoprase quartz)
	Colorado jade (amazonite feldspar)
Greenstone (nephrite jade, New Zealand)	*Fukien jade* (soapstone)
	Honan jade (soapstone)
Imperial jade (fine, gem-quality jadeite jade)	*Indian jade* (aventurine quartz)
	Korea jade (serpentine [bowenite])
Jade (both jadeite and nephrite jade)	*Manchurian jade* (soapstone)
Kidney stone (nephrite)	*Mexican jade* (dyed green calcite)
Maori (nephrite jade, New Zealand)	*New jade* (serpentine [bowenite])
Spinach jade (nephrite jade)	*Oregon jade* (dark green jasper [quartz])
	Soochow jade (serpentine or soapstone)
	Swiss jade (dyed green jasper [quartz])
	Virginia jade (amazonite, variety feldspar)

Opal

Andamooka opal (a type of opal from Andamooka, Australia)	*Gilson opal* (imitation or synthetic)
	Japanese opal (plastic imitation)
Black opal (a rare type of genuine opal with a dark body color)	*Slocum opal* (imitation)

Descriptive Names	Misnomers (And What They Really Are)
Boulder opal (genuine opal in which brown host rock may be seen)	
Fire opal (opal with strong reddish or orangish color, mostly from Mexico)	
Harlequin opal (very rare genuine opal that exhibits a "harlequin" pattern)	
Jelly opal (a transparent type of opal that has a jellylike appearance)	

Ruby

Descriptive Names	Misnomers (And What They Really Are)
African ruby (ruby from Africa)	*Almandine ruby* (garnet)
Burma ruby (ruby from Myanmar [Burma]; the finest considered by connoisseurs to be the most desirable; rare and costly)	*Australian ruby* (garnet)
	Balas ruby (spinel)
	Bohemian ruby (garnet)
	Cape ruby (garnet)
Ceylon ruby (ruby from Sri Lanka [Ceylon])	*Chatham ruby* (synthetic)
	Ramura ruby (synthetic)
Thai ruby (ruby from Thailand)	*Ruby spinel* (spinel)
	Siberian ruby (tourmaline)

Sapphire

Descriptive Names	Misnomers (And What They Really Are)
Australian sapphire (sapphire from Australia)	*Brazilian sapphire* (blue tourmaline; Brazil also has sapphire, called simply sapphire)
Burmese sapphire (sapphire from Myanmar [Burma]; in fine quality, rare and expensive)	*Chatham sapphire* (synthetic)
	Lux sapphire (iolite)
Ceylon sapphire (sapphire from Sri Lanka [Ceylon]; lighter blue than Burmese; fine quality also rare and expensive)	*Water sapphire* (iolite)
Kashmir sapphire (sapphire from Kashmir; fine-quality stones considered by connoisseurs to be the finest; rare and costly)	
Montana, or Yogo, sapphire (sapphire from Montana)	
Oriental sapphire (old term to denote "genuine")	
Thai sapphire (sapphire from Thailand)	

Descriptive Names	Misnomers (And What They Really Are)
Topaz	
Precious (imperial) topaz (usually fine apricot orange)	*Madeira topaz* (citrine quartz)
	Occidental topaz (citrine quartz)*
	Palmeira topaz (citrine quartz)
	Rio topaz (citrine quartz)
	Saffranite topaz (citrine quartz)
	Scottish topaz (citrine quartz)
	Smokey topaz (smokey quartz)
	Spanish topaz (citrine quartz)

*Much of the citrine quartz seen on the market today is produced by heating the purple variety (amethyst). This heating alters the color from purple to shades of yellow, yellow-brown, or golden yellow.

Other Names You Might See

Names	What They Really Are
Aquagem	Light blue synthetic spinel
California moonstone	Chalcedony quartz
California turquoise	Variscite
Chortanite	Imitation tanzanite (YAG)
Cortanite	Imitation tanzanite (YAG)
Esmeralda	Green tourmaline
Forsterite	Imitation tanzanite
German lapis	Dyed blue jasper (quartz)
Goldstone	Artificial glass with copper crystals
Imperial yu stone (*yu* is the Chinese word for jade)	Fine green aventurine quartz
Japanese amethyst	Synthetic amethyst
Oriental chrysoberyl	Yellow-green sapphire
Oriental topaz	Yellow sapphire
Rose zircon	Synthetic pink spinel
South Sea cat's-eye	Operculum, "door" of a univalve shellfish
Swiss lapis	Dyed blue jasper (quartz)
Tsavolite	Imitation tsavorite (synthetic corundum)

CHAPTER SEVEN

Buying Colored Gems

When you go to buy colored gemstones today, you will find your-self immersed in color—every hue, every shade of the spectrum. There has never been a more exciting time to search for a colored gem because there have never been so many alternatives.

Today you will find "new" gems only recently discovered: emerald green garnets (tsavorite), blue and green tanzanite (technically, the green variety should be called green zoisite, the mineral name for this gemstone, since *blue* zoisite is what we know as "tanzanite"), and "neon" tourma-lines from Paraiba, Brazil (also called Hetorita, after the man who dis-covered them) in blue and green shades never seen before. Even diamond can be seen in a wide variety of natural "fancy" colors, some at very "fancy" prices (see *Diamonds: The Antoinette Matlins Buying Guide*).

Whatever color you prefer, and whatever your budget, there is a sparkling natural gem awaiting your discovery. If you want an emerald green stone but can't afford a fine emerald, you might choose a green gar-net (tsavorite), a green tourmaline, chrome diopside, or green tanzanite; if you like ruby red, but can't afford ruby, you might choose from red spinel, red tourmaline, or red garnet; if you prefer blue, choices now include blue spinel, iolite, tourmaline, and tanzanite. And we've just begun to scratch the surface.

Before getting started, just remember that with so many gemstones available in similar colors, the risk of erroneous identification increases; bas-ing identification on color alone is too often the cause. Unfortunately, most people still don't realize how many gems look alike in color. And even professionals in the trade can be misled or caught off-guard. Increasingly, inexpensive gems are mixed in with parcels of more costly gems of similar color and passed off as the more costly gem. These can get passed on to unsuspecting manufacturers, designers, jewelers, and, thus, ultimately to consumers. This is just one more reason why it is especially important to seek a knowledgeable, reputable jeweler when purchasing any colored gemstone, and to verify the authenticity of any significant gem purchase with an independent gem-testing laboratory or gemologist-appraiser.

In the following pages I will present some of the most popular gemstone alternatives by color; a table that indicates the effect of treatments on gemstone value; a list of gemstones that are not routinely treated; and a guide to how they compare in terms of price, availability, and wearability. Then the gems will be discussed individually in chapter 8.

Gem Alternatives by Color

Color Family	Popular Name of Stone	Gem Family
Red— *from red to shades of pink*	Andalusite—pink to reddish brown	Andalusite
	Diamond*—all shades of pink and red	Diamond
	Garnet—several red color varieties	
	Almandine—violet to pure red	Garnet
	Malaya—brownish red to orangy red	Garnet
	Pyrope—brownish red to red	Garnet
	Rhodolite—red to violet	Garnet
	Kunzite—violet-pink to pink-violet	Spodumene
	Morganite—pink to orange-pink	Beryl
	Pink sapphire—pinkish red	Corundum
	Red "emerald"—red	Beryl
	Rose quartz—pure pink	Quartz
	Rubellite—red to violet-red and pink	Tourmaline
	Ruby—bluish red to orange-red	Corundum
	Scapolite—light red	Scapolite
	Spinel—red to brownish red and pink	Spinel
	Sunstone—rich red to orange-red	Feldspar
	Zircon—brownish red to deep, dark red	Zircon
Orange	Diamond*—various shades including yellow-orange to brownish orange	Diamond
	Garnet—a few orange varieties	
	Hessonite—orange-brown to brown-orange	Garnet
	Malaya—red-orange to orangy brown	Garnet
	Spessartite—orange to red-orange to brown-orange	Garnet
	Morganite—pale orange to orangy pink	Beryl
	Padparadscha sapphire—pinkish orange	Corundum
	Scapolite—orange	Scapolite

Spinel—brown to orange   Spinel
Sunstone—rich orange to orange-red   Feldspar
Topaz—brownish orange, yellow-orange,   Topaz
   pinkish orange
Tourmaline—all shades of orange   Tourmaline
Zircon—orange to golden brown   Zircon

Yellow	Beryl (heliodor)—golden yellow	Beryl
	Chrysoberyl—yellow, yellow-green, yellow-brown	Chrysoberyl
	Citrine—yellow to yellow-brown	Quartz
	Diamond*—all shades of yellow to chartreuse	Diamond
	Garnet—a couple of yellow varieties	
	Andradite—honey yellow to greenish yellow	Garnet
	Grossularite—yellow to greenish yellow	Garnet
	to brownish yellow	
	Sapphire—yellow	Corundum
	Scapolite—yellow	Scapolite
	Sphene—green-yellow to golden yellow to brown	Sphene
	Sunstone—orangy yellow, yellow, greenish yellow	Feldspar
	Topaz—brownish yellow to yellow	Topaz
	Tourmaline—all shades	Tourmaline
	Zircon—yellow to yellow-brown	Zircon

Green	Alexandrite—daylight: bluish to blue-green;	Chrysoberyl
	artificial light: violet-red	
	Apatite—green to blue-green	Apatite
	Chrome diopside—green to yellow-green to	Diopside
	blue-green	
	Diamond*—blue-green to yellow-green to gray-green	Diamond
	Emerald—yellowish green to bluish green	Beryl
	Garnet—a couple of green varieties	
	Demantoid—yellow-green to emerald green	Garnet
	Tsavorite—yellowish green to bluish green	Garnet
	Peridot—yellow-green to green	Peridot
	Sapphire—yellow-green to blue-green to gray-green	Corundum
	Scapolite—greenish gray	Scapolite
	Sphene—grass green to yellow-green	Sphene
	Sunstone—yellowish, grayish, brownish green	Feldspar
	Tanzanite—gray-green to blue-green	Zoisite
	Tourmaline—several green color varieties	
	Chrome—rich green to slightly yellow-green	Tourmaline
	Paraiba—light to deep green to blue-green	Tourmaline
	Verdelite—all shades of green	Tourmaline
	Zircon—green to yellow-green to gray-green	Zircon

Blue	Apatite—blue to gray-blue to greenish blue	Apatite
	Aquamarine—blue to blue-green	Beryl
	Diamond*—all shades	Diamond
	Iolite—violet to gray-blue	Iolite
	Sapphire—cornflower blue to greenish blue to inky blue	Corundum
	Spinel—blue, gray-blue, greenish blue	Spinel
	Tanzanite—violet-blue	Zoisite
	Topaz—blue to blue-green	Topaz
	Tourmaline—a couple of blue color varieties	
	Indicolite—inky blue, greenish blue	Tourmaline
	Paraiba—intense blue to violet-blue to green-blue	Tourmaline
	Zircon—pastel blue	Zircon
Violet	Amethyst—lilac to violet to reddish purple to brownish purple	Quartz
	Benitoite—blue to violet-blue to gray-blue	Benitoite
	Diamond*—all shades	Diamond
	Kunzite—pinkish violet to red-violet	Spodumene
	Morganite—pinkish violet	Beryl
	Paraiba—violet to blue-violet	Tourmaline
	Rhodolite—red-violet	Garnet
	Sapphire—purple to violet	Corundum
	Scapolite—violet-blue, to greenish to bluish gray, lilac to violet	Scapolite
	Spinel—grayish violet to pure purple	Spinel

*For information on colored diamonds see *Diamonds: The Antoinette Matlins Buying Guide*.

The Effect of Treatments on the Value of Gemstones

The following table provides an indication of price adjustment for *natural* versus *treated* ruby, sapphire, and emerald. Keep in mind that untreated sapphire and ruby from certain locations, such as Burma or Kashmir, command a premium greater than indicated. Also, note that there are rare gems of exceptional quality above the extra fine rating, and such stones will command a much greater premium if untreated.

How Treatments Affect Prices of Colored Gems*

Emerald	GOOD	FINE	EXTRA FINE
Untreated	+10% to +25%	+25% to +50%	+50% and up
Slight treatment	0%	0%	0%
Moderate treatment	–5% to –10%	–10% to –15%	–15% to –25%
Extensive treatment	–15% to –20%	–20% to –25%	–25% to –35%
Ruby			
Unheated	+5% to +20%	+20% to +35%	+35% to +50% and up
Moderate heat	0%	0%	0%
High heat with			
slight glass residue	–5%	–5% to –10%	–10% to –15%
moderate glass residue	–5% to –10%	–10% to –15%	–15% to –20%
extensive glass residue	–15% to –20%	–20% to –25%	–25% to –35%
Glass-filled cavity	–10% to –50%	–10% to –50%	–10% to –50%
Sapphire			
Unheated	+5% to +10%	+10% to +20%	+20% to +30% and up
Heated	0%	0%	0%
Oiled (no data; often goes undetected)			

*The information presented above is based on information from several sources, including *The Guide* (Gemworld International) and *JCK Magazine*.

The Rarest of Them All—The Natural Gems

There has been so much focus on the extensive use of treatments to enhance gems that it is easy to forget that there are also natural gems: those that have not been artificially enhanced in any way. Within every gemstone family there is the occasional beauty that is just as nature made it. Unfortunately, as I discussed earlier, sometimes we cannot distinguish what is natural from what is not. Such is the case with blue topaz, for example. Blue topaz does occur naturally, in lovely pastel shades. It is one of nature's rarest and loveliest gems, but alas, we do not yet have the means to definitively distinguish what is natural from what has been irradiated. Thus, regardless of its rarity and true preciousness (and value), it commands a very small price.

There are also natural rubies, sapphires, and emeralds. Most are not the color and clarity we've come to expect (from the standards applied to the treated gems), but we are starting to see interest in a wider range of qualities, especially for stones in the lighter shades of color. And exceptionally fine-quality rubies, sapphires, and emeralds also exist. Fortunately, where ruby, sapphire, and emerald are concerned, it is usually possible to distinguish the natural from the treated, and as the natural stones become even rarer and rarer, prices are starting to reflect their preciousness, as you've seen in the table on page 87.

There is yet another group of gems about which little has been said until recently: gemstones and gemstone families that are not routinely treated to alter color or clarity at this time. When you buy one of the gemstones listed in the chart below, the color is generally natural, and in most cases these gemstones are not enhanced in any way. Included in the list are many beautiful choices in a rainbow of colors. If you are not familiar with them, there is more information in the following chapters. Whatever your color preference and budget, if you seek something truly "natural," you should be able to find the right gem from this list. If jewelers in your area don't have what you want, they can contact the American Gem Trade Association (AGTA) to arrange to get stones for you to see.

---

*Gemstones That Are Not Routinely Enhanced**

Alexandrite	Iolite	Tourmaline (rare
Andalusite	Moonstone	chrome green
Chrysoberyl	Fire opal	variety and cat's-
(all colors)	Peridot	eye tourmaline)
Chrysoprase	Spinel (all colors)	Zircon (brown and
Garnet (all colors)	Tanzanite (green)	green varieties)
Hematite		

*The color of these gems is normally natural. In rare instances, surface-reaching fractures or cavities may be filled with oil, wax, or resin.

How to Use the Following Guides

The purpose of the following price guides is twofold: to help you understand how prices for different gems in a given color compare with one another; and to demonstrate how significant the price range might be for a given type of stone, so that you will have a clearer understanding of the importance of quality differences.

The guides can be especially useful—and help you avoid mistakes—if you follow these steps:

- *Decide what color you want in a gem, and then make a list of the gems available in that color.* If you want an emerald green gem, for example, and can't afford emerald itself, you would use the guide to see what other similarly colored emerald green gems are available: tsavorite garnet, chrome tourmaline, green tourmaline, or green sapphire, for example.

- *Compare their prices* to get a sense of the relative cost of each. In comparing prices for these green gems, you would immediately see that tsavorite garnet is the most expensive (but still much more affordable than emerald), chrome tourmaline is next in cost, then green tourmaline, and finally the most affordable, green sapphire.

- *Note availability* to determine how easy or difficult it might be to locate the particular gem you think you want. In this example, you would see that of the choices, green sapphire is not as readily available as several other choices and might be difficult to find.

- *Note the range in price* for the stones that interest you. *The larger the price range in a given stone, the more critical any differences in quality become.* A wide price variance would indicate that you must be especially careful to spend time comparing and learning about the stone, developing an eye to spot subtle differences in quality.

- *Read about each gem individually.* Now turn to chapter 8 and read about each of the gems you're considering individually. You may find that there is something about the stone or its history, mythology, or wearability that makes it an even more interesting choice for you. Here you will also learn if there is anything special you need to know, to look for, or to look out for as you shop.

Now, you're ready to embark on a sparkling search. But always remember: *being genuine doesn't mean a stone is a "gem" or that it is "valuable."* There are genuine rubies, sapphires, and emeralds that can be bought for a couple of dollars per carat, and some you couldn't pay me to take! A gem must be beautiful and rare, attributes that are related to *quality.* The finer the quality, the more beautiful, and the more rare. The quality of the individual stone is what determines whether or not it is a "gem," and it is the *quality* that determines its value. The range in price for any colored gemstone is directly related to quality differences—and it can be enormous. Be sure you have read chapter 4 carefully, and understand the factors that determine quality before making any decision.

After reading these chapters, you will know what to ask the jeweler to show you. But don't forget to do a lot of window-shopping, looking, and asking questions until you really have developed a feel for that particular stone and its market.

Price Guides to Popular Gems

The prices quoted in these price guides are for faceted gemstones unless otherwise noted. Cabochon-cut stones often cost less. Prices shown are for good to extra fine quality. Gems used in mass-produced jewelry sold in many jewelry stores are often of commercial quality and may cost significantly less than the prices indicated here. Also, it is rare to find gems sold by jewelry retailers that exceed the prices shown for extra fine quality. Rare gems in exceptionally fine quality and rare stones of unusual size can sell for much more than the prices indicated here. If the price of a gem you are considering is higher than what I indicate, I strongly recommend taking extra steps to confirm its exceptional quality before purchase; in some cases I would recommend having the seller obtain a quality grading report from a laboratory such as the American Gemological Laboratories (AGL) or the American Gem Trade Association (AGTA) Gemological Testing Center.

The prices shown for gems that are routinely treated or enhanced in some way—ruby, sapphire, emerald, topaz, tourmaline, and so on— reflect prices for treated material (showing evidence of "moderate" treatment). For natural gemstones, or heavily treated stones, see price adjustment chart on page 87.

Guide to Popular Gems and Their Prices*

Family	Popular Name	Color(s)	Approx. Retail Cost Per Carat	Brilliance	Wearability	Availability
Ammolite	Ammolite or ammonite	Orange, red, green, yellow, blue, purple	per carat: $400–5,000	Good	Poor to good	Most colors: good; blue and purple: poor
Andalusite	Poor man's alexandrite	Changes color from grayish green to reddish brown, emerald green to bright yellow	1 to under 5 cts: $75–450 5 to under 10 cts: $180–600	Good	Good	Large: poor; smaller: fair
Apatite	Apatite	Various shades of blue and green varieties	1 to under 3 cts: $60–300 3 to under 5 cts: $75–450	Fair	Fair, soft, scratches easily	Good
Benitoite	Benitoite	Blue, violetish blue, bluish violet	½ to under 1 ct: $750–2,500 1 to under 2 cts: $1,250–4,250 2 to under 3 cts: $2,000–6,250	Very good	Fair to good	1 ct: good; larger: fair to poor
Beryl[1]	Aquamarine	Pastel blue to medium deep blue	1 to under 5 cts: $75–1,500 5 to under 10 cts: $225–1,500	Good	Good	Good
	Golden beryl (heliodor)	Yellow, brownish yellow	1 to under 5 cts: $75–180 5 to under 10 cts: $105–300	Good	Good	Good
	Green beryl	Pastel grayish green to yellowish green or bluish green	1 to under 5 cts: $45–375 5 to under 10 cts: $60–600	Good	Good	Good
	Emerald[2]	Yellow-green to blue-green	1 to under 2 cts: $900–11,000 2 to under 4 cts: $1,250–15,200	Fair to good	Fair to good	Very fine Colombian: rare; others: good

*Prices compiled from *The Guide*, Gemworld International, Inc., and adjusted to retail.

[1] Beryl also comes in green (different from emerald green), lilac, salmon, and orange. Most are still not readily available, but some, such as the lovely orange variety, can be found for under $75 per carat and offer excellent value.

[2] Cabochon-cut rubies, sapphires, and emeralds usually cost much less; the finest gems can cost much more.

Chart continues on next page.

Family	Popular Name	Color(s)	Approx. Retail Cost Per Carat	Brilliance	Wearability	Availability
Beryl (*cont.*)	Morganite	Pink to orange-pink	1 to under 5 cts: $30–300 5 to under 10 cts: $75–600	Good	Good	Fine: rare; medium: good
	Red beryl[3] (Red Emerald™)	Light to deep orangish red to purplish red	under 1 ct: $300–15,000 1+ to 3+ cts: $2,000–40,000	Fair to good	Fair to good	Very fine: rare; medium: good
Chrysoberyl	Alexandrite	Changes from greenish in daylight to reddish in incandescent light	½ to under 2 cts: $2,100–16,000 2 to under 5 cts: $3,750–28,000	Good	Excellent	Large: poor; small: fair
	Chrysoberyl	Yellow to yellow-brown to yellow-green	1 to under 5 cts: $60–300 5 to under 10 cts: $120–750	Good	Excellent	Fair
	Precious cat's-eye	Greenish to brownish yellow with "eye" effect	1 to under 3 cts: $900–5,750 3 to under 5 cts: $1,800–6,400	Negligible	Excellent	Fair to good
Corundum	Ruby[2]	Red to bluish or purplish red to yellow-red	½ to under 1 ct: $675–7,000 1 to under 2 cts: $975–12,000 2 to under 4 cts: $1,250–21,500	Fair to good	Excellent	Fine, natural color: rare; others: good
	Blue sapphire[2]	Bright blue to inky blue	½ to under 1 ct: $225–2,175 1 to under 2 cts: $450–8,400 2 to under 4 cts: $975–9,800	Good	Excellent	Natural color, Burmese and Kashmir: rare; others: good
	Colorless sapphire	White (colorless)	½ to under 1 ct: $30–180 1 to under 2 cts: $60–240	Good	Very good	Fair
	Green sapphire	Clear green to brownish or bluish green	1 to under 3 cts: $75–750 3 to under 5 cts: $225–1,050	Good	Excellent	Clear green: rare; others: good
	Pink sapphire	Light to very dark pink (almost red)	1 to under 2 cts: $750–2,500 2 to under 3 cts: $975–3,250	Good	Excellent	Good in sizes under 1 ct
	Yellow sapphire	Yellow (most are heat-treated; natural yellow usually less brilliant)	1 to under 5 cts: $180–1,500 5 to under 10 cts: $600–2,100	Good	Excellent	Large: poor; others: fair

[2]Cabochon-cut rubies, sapphires, and emeralds usually cost much less; finest gems can cost much more.

Feldspar	Labradorite	Deep gray-blue to brownish blue with strong iridescent play of color	16" strand of 8mm beads: $165–220 1 to under 5 cts: $16–110	Not applicable	Not applicable	Good
	Moonstone	Milky white to blue-white	1 to under 5 cts: $21–195 5 to under 20 cts: $30–180	Not applicable	Good	White: good; blue: fair
	Sunstone[4]	Red, orange, yellow, deep blue, green	under 1 ct: $75–2,500 1 to under 5 cts: $120–2,500	Fair to good	Good	Small sizes: good; others: fair
Garnet	Almandine (common garnet)	Purplish red to pure red	1 to under 5 cts: $15–60 5 to under 10 cts: $24–90	Fair to good	Good	Fair
	Demantoid	Yellow-green to emerald green	1 to under 2 cts: $1,200–8,000 2 to under 3 cts: $2,500–12,000	Very good	Good	Good
	Grossularite	Yellow to yellowish green to yellowish brown	1 to under 5 cts: $60–300 5 to under 10 cts: $150–675	Fair to good	Good	Good
	Malaya	Pink-orange to brownish red	1 to under 5 cts: $60–300 5 to under 10 cts: $150–675	Good	Good	Poor
	Pyrope (common garnet)	Yellowish red to dark red	1 to under 5 cts: $15–60 5 to under 20 cts: $24–150	Fair to good	Good	Good
	Rhodolite	Red-violet	1 to under 5 cts: $30–180 5 to under 20 cts: $75–450	Good	Good	Good
	Spessartite	Brownish orange to reddish brown to brownish red	1 to under 5 cts: $12–90 5 to under 30 cts: $36–225	Good	Good	Good
	Mandarin	Intense orange to fiery reddish orange	1 to under 5 cts: $240–1,250 5 to under 10 cts: $600–1,875	Fair to very good	Good	Large: rare; others: good
	Tsavorite	Yellowish green to bluish green	1 to under 2 cts: $540–2,000 2 to under 3 cts: $1,350–4,000 3 to under 5 cts: $2,025–6,750	Good	Good	Good

Chart continues on next page.

[3] Prices are based on information provided by www.redemerald.com.
[4] Bicolor, tricolor, and color-change sunstones also occur but are rare. Prices for these are much higher than indicated for other colors of sunstone.

Family	Popular Name	Color(s)	Approx. Retail Cost Per Carat	Brilliance	Wearability	Availability
Iolite	Iolite	Violet-blue to gray-blue	1 to under 5 cts: $60–300 5 to under 10 cts: $135–375	Good	Fair	Fair
Peridot (olivine)	Peridot	Yellow-green to deep green to rich chartreuse	1 to under 5 cts: $60–300 5 to under 10 cts: $90–555	Fair to good	Fair, will scratch easily	Large: poor; smaller: good
Quartz	Amethyst	Purple, reddish purple to brownish purple	1 to under 5 cts: $9–90 5 to under 10 cts: $15–120 10 to under 25 cts: $18–135	Fair to good	Good	Very good
	Ametrine	Shades of yellow and purple in same stone	1 to under 5 cts: $9–30 5 under 20 cts: $15–60	Good	Good	Good
	Citrine	Yellow to yellow-brown	1 to under 5 cts: $9–66 5 to under 25 cts: $15–90	Good	Good	Good
	Rose quartz & Smokey quartz	Pure pink; some murky; some clear, transparent; brown shades	most sizes: $6–30 per stone	Good	Good	Good
Spinel	Blue spinel	Medium gray-blue to deep blue to violet	1 to under 3 cts: $90–1,375 3 to under 5 cts: $120–2,000	Good	Very good	Good
	Pink spinel	Lively or bright pink to brownish pink	1 to under 3 cts: $150–1,350 3 to under 5 cts: $225–1,500	Very good	Very good	Fair
	Red spinel	Red to brownish red	1 to under 3 cts: $225–1,375 3 to under 5 cts: $300–2,500	Very good	Very good	Ruby red: poor; others: good
Spodumene	Kunzite	Lilac, violet, pink	1 to under 5 cts: $18–240 5 to under 20 cts: $75–270	Good	Poor for rings	Good
Topaz	Blue topaz	Blue	1 to under 5 cts: $3–24 5 to under 20 cts: $9–36	Good	Fair	Good
	Imperial topaz	Golden with pinkish/reddish overtone	1 to under 3 cts: $120–1,650 3 to under 5 cts: $180–1,500	Good	Fair	Fair to good except in very large sizes

Topaz *(cont.)*	Pink topaz	Pink (red also available, but very rare and much more expensive)	1 to under 3 cts: $180–1,450 3 to under 5 cts: $180–1,500	Good	Fair	Fair to good
	Yellow/golden topaz	Yellow/golden (no pink/red overtone)	1 to under 5 cts: $105–600 5 to under 20 cts: $180–900	Good	Good	Good
Tourmaline	Chrome	Deep green	1 to under 3 cts: $225–1,500 3 to under 5 cts: $750–1,565	Good	Fair to good	Poor
	Indicolite	Inky blue to blue-green	1 to under 5 cts: $150–1,200 5 to under 10 cts: $240–1,500	Good	Fair to good	Good
	Paraiba (neon)	Wide range of "neon" blue, green, blue-green, and purplish blue	under 1 ct: $1,200–10,000 1 to under 3 cts: $4,500–36,000	Excellent	Fair to good	Under 1 ct: fair; over 1 ct in fine quality: scarce
	Pink	Pink or rose	1 to under 5 cts: $75–600 5 to under 10 cts: $150–780	Good	Fair to good	Good
	Rubellite	Red to violet	1 to under 5 cts: $210–795 5 to under 10 cts: $255–1,050	Good	Fair to good	Good
	Verdelite (green)	Green—all shades except chrome tourmaline	1 to under 3 cts: $90–480 3 to under 5 cts: $105–600 5 to under 20 cts: $135–1,200	Good	Fair to good	Good
	Golden	Yellow, orange, and brown varieties	1 to under 5 cts: $75–600	Good	Fair to good	Fair
	Bicolor, tricolor	Red/black, red/green, red/green/colorless	1 to under 5 cts: $60–750 5 to under 10 cts: $135–900	Good	Fair to good	Good
Zircon	Zircon	Pastel blue (usually heat-treated)	1 to under 5 cts: $45–450 5 to under 10 cts: $105–900	Good	Fair—Zircon is not recommended for rings	Large: poor
		Green to yellow-green	1 to under 5 cts: $30–150 5 to under 10 cts: $90–180	Good	Good	Good
		Colorless (usually heat-treated)	Comparable to green	Good	Good	Good

Chart continues on next page.

Family	Popular Name	Color(s)	Approx. Retail Cost Per Carat	Brilliance	Wearability	Availability
Zircon (*cont.*)	**Zircon** (*cont.*)	Orange to golden brown	Comparable to green	Good	Fair— Zircon is not recommended for rings	Good
		Red to brownish red	Prices unknown (rare)	Good		True red: poor; other reds: good
		Yellow to yellow-brown	Comparable to green	Good		Good
Zoisite	**Tanzanite (blue-violet)**	Strong blue to weak violet, blue-violet	1 to under 3 cts: $525–1,450 3 to under 5 cts: $750–1,450 5 to under 20 cts: $825–1,500	Good	Poor for rings	Good
	Green tanzanite	Blue-green to gray-green	1 to under 3 cts: $1600–5,000	Good	Good	Small: fair; large: poor

Opal Retail Price Guide*
Approximate Retail Cost *Per Carat*

There are numerous varieties of opals and wide ranges in quality. Quality differences are often difficult for the amateur to distinguish, but these may significantly affect price. The following prices provide only a guide. For more detailed information, see Selected Readings.

Popular Opal Varieties

Type	Size	Good	Fine	Extra Fine
White base, gray base, jelly opal	1 to under 15 cts	$30–75	$75–255	$255–750
Crystal	1 to under 15 cts	$60–180	$180–1,250	$1,250–7,250
Semi-crystal	1 to under 15 cts	$36–120	$120–600	$600–2,250
Semi-black	1 to under 15 cts	$120–480	$480–2,250	$2,250–6,000
Fire (faceted)	5 to under 10 cts	$75–270	$270–525	$525–900

Black and Crystal Black Opal

Color	Size	Good	Fine	Extra Fine
Red-orange	1 to under 10 cts	$300–1,750	$1,750–8,000	$8,000–25,000
	10 to under 15 cts	$300–1,625	$1,625–7,000	$7,000–20,000
Green-blue	1 to under 15 cts	$180–750	$750–3,500	$3,500–9,200

Boulder Opal—Price per stone

	Size	Good	Fine	Extra Fine
Small	1 to under 5 cts	$90–2,750	$2,750–6,600	$6,600–13,200
Medium	5 to under 10 cts	$1,050–3,000	$3,000–12,000	$12,000–22,000
Large	10 to under 15 cts	$1,200–5,500	$5,500–16,400	$16,400–50,000
Very large	15 to under 30 cts	$1,500–6,600	$6,600–22,000	$22,000–80,000

Opal Triplets—Price per piece

Size	Good	Fine	Extra Fine
8x6 mm	$21–36	$48	$84
10x8 mm	$39–84	$96	$144
12x10 mm	$57–114	$150	$222
14x10 mm	$78–165	$210	$315

*Prices compiled from *The Guide*, Gemworld International, Inc., and adjusted to retail.

Synthetic Gemstone Retail Price Guide

(Prices are compiled from *The Guide*, Gemworld International, Inc., and adjusted to retail.)

Common Synthetics

Prices are *per stone* in U.S. dollars.

Shape	Cubic Zirconia (CZ)	Synthetic Spinel	Synthetic Sapphire	Synthetic Spinel Triplet
Oval				
8x6 mm	$6	$9	$9	$18
10x8 mm	$9	$12	$15	$26
12x10 mm	$12	$15	$18	$32
Round				
4 mm	$2.25	$3	$6	$9
6 mm	$3.75	$6	$9	$18
8 mm	$6	$9	$12	$24

Flux Grown Synthetics

Prices are per carat in U.S. dollars and are for all shapes.

Gemstone	Gem+ (flawless)	Gem Quality (eye clean)	Fine (slightly included)	A (moderately included)
Chatham created emerald (5–10 carats)		$675	$525	$300
Chatham created ruby (5–10 carats)		$645	$450	$300
Chatham created blue, pink, and padparadscha sapphire and alexandrite (5–10 carats)*			$450	
Ramaura™ cultured ruby (3–5 carats)	$900	$600	$450	$300
Empress™ cultured emerald (5–10 carats)	$900	$600	$480	$300
Nicholas™ created alexandrite (all weights)		$300		

*Alexandrite and sapphire are available in only one quality—fine.

Hydrothermal and Pulled Synthetics

Prices are per carat in U.S. dollars.

Gemstone	Promotional	Fine	Gem	All Qualities
Kimberley® created emerald (hydrothermal; all weights)	$150	$225	$300	
Kimberley® created ruby, sapphire, and padparadscha sapphire (pulled method; all weights)			$150	
Kimberley® created alexandrite (all weights)			$210	
Lannyte lab-grown ruby and rose sapphire (round)*				
2+mm				$195
4+mm				$150
6+mm				$90
Lannyte lab-grown alexandrite (round)*				
4+mm				$150
6.5+mm				$120
8+mm				$105
Lannyte lab-grown emerald (square)*				
4–4.5mm				$180
5–6.5mm				$150
7–10mm				$120

*Add $6 per carat for radiant, princess, and cushion cuts.

Recrystallized Ruby, Recrystallized Sapphire, and Blue and Green YAG (Yttrium Aluminum Garnet)

Prices are per carat in U.S. dollars.

Larger than 1 carat	Top Quality
Recrystallized ruby	$630
Recrystallized sapphire	$690
Blue and green YAG	$90

Gilson Lab-Created Opal

Prices are per carat in U.S. dollars and are for all shapes.

All Weights	All Qualities
White Gilson opal	$135
Crystal Gilson opal	$150
Black Gilson opal	$195

Lannyte Emerald Doublets

Prices are per carat in U.S. dollars.

Shape	Top Quality Only
Round	
4 mm	$200
8 mm	$225
12 mm	$250
Emerald cut	
4x6 mm	$200
8x10 mm	$225
10x12 mm	$250
Oval	
4x6 mm	$200
8x10 mm	$225
12x14 mm	$250

CHAPTER EIGHT

Colorful Choices in Colored Gemstones

The Big Three—Emerald, Ruby, and Sapphire

Emerald

Emerald is a green variety of the mineral beryl. One of the rarest members of the beryl family, it is one of the most highly prized of all the gems. There is only one member of the beryl family that is rarer—the *red* variety, also known as Red Emerald™. Aside from being the birthstone for May, it was historically believed to bestow on its wearer faithfulness and unchanging love, and was thought to enable the wearer to forecast events.

Contrary to popular belief, emerald is *not soft*. It ranks 7½ to 8 on Mohs' scale—an internationally recognized standard that ranks hardness on a scale from 1 to 10, with 1 being the softest and 10 the hardest. It is more fragile than other varieties of beryl and other gems, however, because it is more brittle and under more stress from fractures resulting from the violent geologic conditions under which it formed. This is why it is important to exercise care when you are wearing and handling emerald.

The highest-quality emerald has the color of fresh young green grass—an almost pure spectral green, possibly with a very faint blue tint. Flawless emeralds are so rare that they are immediately suspect; thus, "flaws" have come to serve as "fingerprints" of genuineness. Connoisseurs seek fine emeralds from Colombia, which is known for its intensely rich, vivid-colored emeralds. Colombia is one of the most important emerald sources historically, but other sources now include Afghanistan, Brazil, India, Pakistan, Russia, and Zambia. It is also worth noting that a new emerald discovery in the United States, in Hiddenite, North Carolina, has produced some major crystals with fine color and clarity, and may provide an important new source of fine emerald.

Because of emerald's popularity and value, imitations are abundant. Glass, manufactured complete with "flaws," and doublets or triplets, like "aquamarine emeralds" and "Tecla emeralds" (see chapter 6), are often encountered. New products such as the "Lannyte emerald doublet" are also entering the market; when properly represented, they can make an interesting jewelry choice, but a second or third party may fail to mention that they are doublets.

Also, fine synthetic emeralds are being produced (see chapter 5) that are indistinguishable from the natural with the eye alone. They not only look like natural emerald in their outward appearance, but the internal characteristics can so closely resemble the natural that it is sometimes necessary to send the stone to a major gem-testing laboratory to determine whether it is natural or synthetic. These synthetics are not inexpensive themselves, except by comparison with a genuine emerald of equivalent quality.

Techniques to enhance color and reduce the visibility of flaws are also frequently used. A common practice is to fill surface-reaching cracks with oil (sometimes tinted green)—a practice that goes back to early Greek times. Today emeralds are oiled by use of a vacuum/heat technology. This is a widely accepted trade practice, since it is actually good for the stone in light of its fragile nature. Oiling hides some of the whitish flaws, which are actually cracks, filling the cracks so they become less visible. The oil becomes an integral part of the emerald unless it is subjected to some type of degreasing procedure. The development and use of the ultrasonic cleaner has brought to light the extensiveness of this practice. *Never clean emeralds in an ultrasonic cleaner.* (An ionic cleaner is fine for emeralds as well as for all other jewelry.)

A good friend of mine took her heirloom emerald ring to her jeweler for a "really good cleaning." Luckily for the jeweler, she never left the store and was standing right there when the ring was put into the cleaner and removed. She couldn't believe her eyes. She was shocked by the loss of color and the sudden appearance of more flaws. The ultrasonic cleaner had removed the oil that had penetrated the cracks, and an emerald several shades lighter and more visibly flawed emerged. Had she not been there, she would never have believed the jeweler hadn't pulled a switch.

Oiling is considered an acceptable practice, but be sure the price reflects the actual quality of the stone. If necessary, most emeralds can be re-oiled.

Epoxy resin fillers are a recent newcomer, but this treatment is gaining popularity and is now used on many emeralds mined in many parts of the world, including Colombia and Brazil.

As with all highly desired gems, the greater the value and demand, the greater the occurrence of fraudulent practices. Examples of almost every type of technique to simulate emerald can be found: color alteration by using green foil on closed backs; use of synthetics; substitution of less valuable green stones, doublets, or other composites. Therefore, be especially cautious of bargains, deal with reputable jewelers when planning to purchase, and *always* have the purchase double-checked by a qualified gemologist-appraiser. Any very fine emerald purchased today should have a laboratory report or be submitted to a lab to obtain one.

An American Gem Gains World Recognition—Red Emerald™. Gemologists prefer calling this gem *red beryl* or *bixbite* (after Mr. Bixby, the man who discovered it) rather than red "emerald," but whatever the name, it is a beautiful gem and one of the world's rarest.

As I discuss in greater detail later, the beryl family offers us many beautiful gems: the blue variety is known as *aquamarine,* the pink variety as *morganite* (named after the wealthy twentieth-century philanthropist, J.P. Morgan), a colorless variety as *goshenite,* and the deep green variety as *emerald.* There is also a more common variety that occurs in a range of yellow shades that is known simply as *golden beryl* or *yellow beryl.* And another fairly common variety known simply as *green beryl* occurs in a light-to-medium bluish, yellowish, or grayish green.

The only known source of gem-quality red beryl is the United States. The mine is located in the state of Utah, in the Wahwah Mountain range. Red beryl from this mine is marketed under the name Red Emerald™. For years it was known only to collectors, gemologists, and rock hounds; jewelers were unaware of it because there was insufficient supply to meet any significant demand, so it remained obscure. This began to change when a major pocket was discovered in the 1980s, and red beryl is now making its debut in fine jewelry.

Until red beryl became available, the rarest variety of beryl was the deep green variety known as emerald. The red variety is even rarer, and in an effort to communicate its rarity, preciousness, and value, many prefer to call it red "emerald." In fact, apart from its color, it more closely resembles emerald than any other member of the beryl family, especially in terms of internal features such as inclusions and fractures (resulting from the stressful geological conditions under which it is created). In light of this and the fact that it is even rarer than the green variety we call emerald, most people agree that referring to it as "red emerald" most clearly communicates to the lay person what it is. Furthermore, in terms of value, the association to emerald does not create a misleading perception of value or rarity; it is rarer and can be costlier than emerald itself.

Red Emerald™ remains rare in sizes over 2 carats. The world's largest Red Emerald™ weighs 8.03 carats; the second largest weighs 4.50 carats. In sizes up to 2 carats, the price of fine-quality Red Emerald™ can be comparable to fine ruby, and the price often exceeds that of green emerald.

USEFUL FACTS

Emerald Composition: beryllium aluminum silicate   **Hardness**: 7.5–8.0
Weight: light (specific gravity: 2.69–2.76)   **Wearability:** fair to good
Brilliance: moderately high

Ruby

Prized through the ages as, in the words of the Roman historian Pliny, the "gem of gems . . . surpassing all other precious stones in virtue," ruby is the red variety of the mineral corundum. Historically, it has been symbolic of love and passion, considered to be an aid to firm friendship, and believed to ensure beauty. Today's birthstone for July, ruby has a color that ranges from purplish or bluish red to a yellowish red. The finest color is a vivid, almost pure spectral red with a very faint undertone of blue, as seen in Burmese rubies, which are considered the finest among ardent collectors. Other sources of fine ruby are Thailand, Vietnam, Cambodia, Kenya, Tanzania, and Azad Kashmir in Pakistan, and a new deposit was recently discovered in Australia. The ruby is very brilliant and very hard, ranking 9 on Mohs' scale. Ruby is also very durable and wearable—characteristics that make it an unusually fine choice for any piece of jewelry.

Translucent varieties of ruby are also seen, and one variety exhibits a six-ray star effect when cut as a cabochon. This variety is called *star ruby* and is one of nature's most beautiful and interesting gifts. But, as with so many other beautiful gifts once produced only in nature, these lovely gems are now duplicated in synthetic star rubies, and numerous faked star rubies are also the products of human beings' attempts at mimicry.

Here again, remember that the greater the value and demand, the greater the use of techniques to "improve" or to simulate. Among rubies, as among other gemstones, examples of almost every type of deceptive technique can be found—color enhancement, synthesis, substitutes, doublets, triplets, misleading names, and so on. Be especially alert to the possibility of diffusion treatment and oiling of reflective fractures (see chapter 5). The newest laboratory-grown synthetic rubies, like those made by Ramaura and Chatham, are so close to natural ruby in every aspect that many are actually passing for genuine, even among gemologists. When you are getting a very fine, valuable ruby, be sure to verify genuineness with a gemologist who has both many years' experience in colored gems and an astute knowledge of the marketplace today. I would recommend having the jeweler or gemologist also obtain a colored gemstone report from a major gem-testing laboratory.

Here again, be especially cautious of bargains. Deal with reputable jewelers when planning to purchase, and have the purchase double-checked by a qualified gemologist-appraiser.

USEFUL FACTS

Ruby Composition: aluminum oxide   **Hardness**: 9.0
Weight: heavy (specific gravity: 3.97–4.05)   **Wearability**: excellent
Brilliance: high

Sapphire

The "celestial" sapphire—symbol of the heavens, guardian of innocence, bestower of truth and good health, preserver of chastity—is in fact the mineral corundum. While we know it best in its blue variety, which is highly prized, it comes in essentially every color; red corundum is ruby. As with ruby, its sister stone, sapphire is characterized by hardness (9 on Mohs' scale), brilliance, and availability in many beautiful colors, all of which make it probably the most important and most versatile of the gem families.

Blue sapphires can be among the most valuable members of the sapphire family—especially stones from Burma and Kashmir, which are closest to the pure spectral blue. Fine, brilliant, deep blue Burmese sapphires will surely dazzle the eye and the pocketbook, as will the Kashmir, which is a fine velvety-toned deep blue.

The Ceylon (Sri Lanka) sapphires are a very pleasing blue but are a less deep shade than the Burmese or Kashmir, instead tending to fall more on the pastel side.

I am also seeing many Australian sapphires, which are often a dark blue but with a slightly green undertone, as are those from Thailand; both sell for much less per carat. They offer a very affordable alternative to the Burmese, Kashmir, or Ceylon, and can still be very pleasing in their color. Blue sapphires also come from Tanzania, Brazil, Africa, and even the United States. Montana sapphires are very collectible because of their unusual shades of color and because many are *natural* color—that is, not subjected to any treatment. For those who want a gem that is truly "natural," Montana sapphire may be the choice for you.

With sapphire, origin can have a significant effect on price, so if you are purchasing a Kashmir, Burmese, or Ceylon sapphire, that should be noted on the bill of sale.

Like ruby, the blue sapphire may be found in a translucent variety that may show a six-rayed star effect when cut into a cabochon. This variety is known as *star sapphire,* of which there are numerous synthetics (often referred to in the trade as Linde, pronounced *Lin´dee*).

In addition to blue sapphire, we are now beginning to see many other color varieties in the latest jewelry designs—especially yellow and pink (Madagascar has recently emerged as an important source of pink sapphires) and in smaller sizes some beautiful shades of green. These are known as *fancy* sapphires. Compared with the costly blue sapphire and ruby, these stones offer excellent value and real beauty.

A beautiful and rare variety called *padparadscha* (a type of lotus flower) is also in demand. The true padparadscha should exhibit a *pink and orange color simultaneously.* Depending on the richness of color, brilliance, and size, these can be very expensive. A lovely but more common and more affordable variety, available today, is really a rich orange color. It is often sold as padparadscha, but the rarer and more costly gem will always exhibit a strong pink with the orange.

Many sapphires today tend to be too dark, however, because of the presence of too much black and poor cutting (cutting deep for additional weight), but the deep blues can be treated to lighten the color. Inevitably, evidence abounds of every technique known to imitate and improve the perceived quality and value of sapphire (see chapter 5). Be especially alert to the possibility of diffusion treatment, which creates a blue color that is only on the stone's surface, and be aware that oil is being used increasingly to conceal fractures and reflective inclusions. New synthetics are also entering the market in a much wider range of color, including a vivid green color and the lovely orange-pink color of the very rare and costly padparadscha sapphire. Also, watch out for some very convincing doublets—composed of a thin sliver of real sapphire on the top bonded to a *synthetic* bottom—flooding the market. As always, I urge you to be especially cautious of bargains, deal with reputable jewelers, and have your stone double-checked by a qualified gemologist-appraiser.

USEFUL FACTS

Sapphire Composition: aluminum oxide   **Hardness**: 9.0
Weight: heavy (specific gravity: 3.97–4.05)   **Wearability**: excellent
Brilliance: high

Other Popular Colored Gems

Alexandrite

Alexandrite is a fascinating transparent gem that appears grass green in daylight and raspberry red under artificial light. It is a variety of chrysoberyl reputedly discovered in Russia in 1831 on the day the future czar Alexander II reached his majority, and thus it was named in his honor. In Russia, where the national colors also happen to be green and red, it is considered a stone of very good omen. It is also considered Friday's stone, or the stone of "Friday's child."

Unlike other stones, which humankind has known about and admired for thousands of years, alexandrite is a relatively recent gem discovery. Nonetheless, this rare beauty has come into its own; it is sought by connoisseurs and commands very high prices. The primary sources for alexandrite today include Russia, Brazil, Madagascar, and Sri Lanka. While I've seen gem-quality alexandrite in very large sizes (fifteen to twenty carats), they are usually small and are rare in sizes over three carats. A fine three-carat stone can cost $45,000 today. If you see an alexandrite that measures more than half an inch in width, be suspicious of a fake. Alexandrite is a hard, durable stone (8½ on Mohs' scale) and is normally cut in a faceted style, but some cat's-eye–type alexandrites, found in Brazil, are cut as a cabochon to display the eye effect. These are usually small; the largest I've seen was approximately three carats.

Before 1973, there were really no good synthetic alexandrites. While some varieties of synthetic corundum and synthetic spinel were frequently sold as alexandrite, they really didn't look like the real thing but were hard to differentiate, since so few buyers had ever seen genuine stones. They are, however, easy for a gemologist to spot. In 1973, a very good synthetic alexandrite was produced that is not easy to differentiate from natural stones. While a good gemologist today can identify the synthetics, when they first appeared on the market many were mistaken for the real thing. Be especially careful to verify the authenticity of your alexandrite, since it might have been mistakenly identified years ago and passed along to you today as authentic!

USEFUL FACTS

Alexandrite Composition: beryllium aluminum oxide   **Hardness**: 8.50
Weight: heavy (specific gravity: 3.70–3.72)   **Wearability**: excellent
Brilliance: high

Amber

Amber is not a stone but rather amorphous, fossilized tree sap. It was one of the earliest substances used for personal adornment. Modestly decorated pieces of rough amber have been found in Stone Age excavations and are assumed to have been used as amulets and talismans—a use definitely recorded throughout history before, during, and since the ancient Greeks. Because of its beautiful color and the ease with which it could be fashioned, amber quickly became a favorite object of trade and barter and personal adornment. Amber varies from transparent to semi-translucent and from yellow to dark brown in color; occasionally it's seen in reddish and greenish brown tones. In addition, amber can be dyed many colors. Occasionally, one can find "foreign" fragments or insects that were trapped in the amber, which usually increases its value because of the added curiosity factor. The best-known source of amber is in the Baltic region, primarily along the coastlines of Poland and Russia but also in Norway and Denmark. Amber is also found in Canada, the Czech Republic, the Dominican Republic, England, France, Germany, Italy, Mexico, Romania, Sicily, and the United States.

Plastics are the most common amber imitations. But real amber, which is the lightest gem material, may be easily distinguished from most plastic when dropped into a saturated salt solution: amber will float, while plastic sinks. One other commonly encountered "amber" type is "reconstructed" amber—amber fragments compressed under heat to form a larger piece. An expert can differentiate this from the real under magnification.

Amber can be easily tested by touching it in an inconspicuous place with a hot needle (held by tweezers). The whitish smoke that should be produced should smell like burning pine wood, not like medicine or disinfectant. If there is no smoke, but a black mark occurs, then it is *not* amber. Another test is to try to cut a little piece of the amber with a sharp pointed knife, at the drill hole of the bead; if it cuts like wood (producing a shaving), it is *not* amber, which would produce a sharp, crumbly deposit.

With the exception of those pieces possessing special antique value, the value of amber fluctuates with its popularity, which in part is dictated by the fashion industry and the prevalence of yellow and browns in one's wardrobe. Nonetheless, amber has proved itself an ageless gem and will always be loved and admired.

USEFUL FACTS

Amber Composition: organic plant resins	**Hardness**: 2.0–2.5
Weight: very light (specific gravity: 1.05–1.09)	**Wearability**: Good
Brilliance: moderate	

Amethyst

Amethyst, a transparent purple variety of quartz, is one of the most popular of the colored stones. Once believed to bring peace of mind to the wearer, it was also thought to prevent the wearer from getting drunk. If the circle of the sun or moon was engraved thereon, amethyst was believed to prevent death from poison.

Available in shades from light to dark purple, this February birthstone is relatively hard (7 on Mohs' scale), fairly brilliant, and overall a good, versatile, wearable stone, available in plentiful supply even in very large sizes (although large sizes with deep color are now becoming scarce). Amethyst is found in many countries. Some of the finest comes from Bolivia, Brazil, and Russia (which has a slightly reddish undertone to the purple), but it is also found in Australia, Canada, Germany, India, Madagascar, Namibia, Sri Lanka, Uruguay, the United States, and Zambia.

Amethyst is probably one of the most beautiful stones available at a moderate price; buyers should be careful, however, because "fine" amethyst is being produced synthetically today. Most synthetics can be identified by a skilled gemologist.

Amethyst may fade from heat and strong sunshine. Guard your amethyst from these conditions, and it should retain its color indefinitely. We are hearing stories from customers across the country, however, complaining of newly purchased amethyst jewelry fading over just a few months, from *deep purple* to *light lavender.* This should not happen and may result from an unacceptable color treatment. If your stone fades this quickly, return it to your jeweler.

USEFUL FACTS
Amethyst Composition: silicon dioxide   **Hardness**: 7.0
Weight: light (specific gravity: 2.65)   **Wearability**: good
Brilliance: moderate

Ammolite

Ammolite, also called ammonite, is a very interesting, vibrantly colored material that has entered the jewelry scene in recent years. Known to Native Americans of the last century—and believed to be a good-luck stone that would assure wealth and abundance—it has only been since 1981, following the discovery of a new source in Alberta, Canada, that there has been a sufficient supply of fine-quality ammolite to make it available for jewelry.

Ammolite is actually fossilized ammonite, an extinct shellfish that ceased to exist millions of years ago. The fossil has a coiled shape and is popular among fossil collectors. The name is derived from the ancient Egyptian god Ammon, who is depicted with the head of a ram and twisted spiral horns, similar to the coiled shell of the ammonite mollusk.

Ammolite, the gem, results when the calcium in the fossil is replaced with other minerals such as pyrite, iron, calcite, and so on. This is what causes the unusual coloration. Ammolite forms with very distinctive markings. While it resembles black opal in some ways, the surface reveals a unique pattern, an almost "crackled" effect that looks something like a snakeskin. It exhibits a melange of bright colors, including orange, red, green, and yellow. It also occurs with blue and purple, but these colors are rare and highly prized. The finest material exhibits three or more colors and, like fine opal, the color shifts back and forth from one to another as you tilt the stone back and forth.

The *intensity* of color, *range* of color, and *pattern* of color are the most important factors related to quality. The separations between the colors, the dark areas, must also be evaluated. Fine material will have very few or minimal separations, or separations that form a distinct and interesting pattern; if the patterns have special allure, they can increase value. If the separations are pronounced and unsightly, they diminish the value.

Sometimes ammolite is so thin that it is too delicate to use alone in jewelry. Ammolite triplets topped with synthetic spinel are common. Triplets sell for about half the price of natural ammolites. Prices are based on size (number of square millimeters), individuality, and overall quality. Typically, a triplet will range from $200 to $2,500 per stone; natural stones from $400 to $5,000 per stone.

Ammolite is relatively soft (about 4.5 in hardness, but hardness varies) and special care is recommended. Wrap it in a soft cloth or tissue

---

USEFUL FACTS

Ammolite Composition (fossilized ammonite): varies depending on replacement mineral	**Brilliance**: high
	Hardness: varies
Weight: varies	**Wearability**: poor to good

before placing it in a jewelry case, or keep it in a separate compartment to protect it from being scratched. Avoid exposing ammolite to acids, ammonia, hairspray, and perfumes. Clean with a soft brush, using mild soap and water or a pearl cleaner.

Andalusite (Poor Man's Alexandrite)

Andalusite is now offering interesting new possibilities for jewelry. Brazil is the primary source of these fascinating, fairly hard (7 to 7½ on Mohs' scale), and fairly durable stones. Andalusite is very interesting because it may exhibit several colors: an olive green from one direction, a rich reddish brown from another direction, and grayish green from yet another direction. In an emerald cut, it may look primarily green while exhibiting an orange color at the ends of the emerald shape. In a round cut, you may see the green body color with simultaneous flashes of another color. One benefit andalusite has over alexandrite is that you don't have to change the light in which it is being seen to experience its colors; merely changing the perspective does the trick. A rare and sometimes expensive emerald green variety may exhibit a bright yellow simultaneously, or when viewed from different angles. A pink variety does not exhibit this kind of color phenomenon. While andalusite is not readily available yet, it is finding a market, especially among men. Andalusite is found primarily in Brazil and Sri Lanka but other sources include Australia, Canada, Russia, Spain, and the United States.

USEFUL FACTS

Andalusite Composition: aluminum silicate   **Hardness**: 7.0–7.5
Weight: moderately heavy (specific gravity: 3.10–3.2)   **Wearability**: good
Brilliance: moderate

Apatite

Apatite is a lovely stone that occurs in a range of colors including almost every shade of yellow, blue, green, purple, and pink. Unfortunately it is very soft and doesn't wear well. For this reason, it has not been used in jewelry until recently. It has become very popular in the past few years because in its unusual green, blue, and violet colors it is very similar to the newcomer Paraiba tourmaline (see pages 145–147). This very rare variety of tourmaline, discovered in the 1990s, occurs in what has been described as neon colors, colors never seen before in jewelry. The colors are so electric that it became popular overnight. Demand increased while supply dwindled, and prices for Paraiba soared, reaching prices comparable to gem-quality sapphire and emerald! As Paraiba tourmaline exceeded the reach of most people, apatite suddenly came into its own as a gem that is readily available, offering amazingly similar colors and costing a fraction of the price. An apatite in the one- to two-carat size range might cost $200 to 300 per carat compared to $10,000 to $15,000 per carat for a one- to two-carat Paraiba.

Apatite is abundant and is found in many countries, including Myanmar (Burma), Sri Lanka, Brazil, Russia, Canada, East Africa, Sweden, Spain, and Mexico. A yellowish green variety found in Spain is often called *asparagus stone*. In addition to its transparent variety, a more translucent variety is available that may exhibit a strong cat's-eye effect when cut as a cabochon. It is readily available in all sizes, but stones larger than five carats often contain visible inclusions.

While similar in color to Paraiba tourmaline, apatite has much less brilliance and is much softer. Apatite can be used to make very lovely earrings, pendants, and brooches, but I do not recommend it for rings or bracelets because it scratches too easily and its appearance can quickly become dull-looking. Take special precautions to avoid scratching it with harder substances. I recommend keeping apatite jewelry in a separate compartment or section of your jewelry case, and also wrapping it in a soft cloth or tissue to prevent the stones from rubbing against each other or getting scratched by the metal settings. Also keep in mind that if you ever need to repair a piece of jewelry containing apatite, or should you want to remount it, you must advise the jeweler that the stone is apatite and requires special care and handling.

USEFUL FACTS

Apatite Composition: calcium phosphate
Weight: moderately heavy (specific gravity: 3.17–3.23)
Brilliance: moderately high

Hardness: 5.0 (soft)
Wearability: fair (poor in rings/ bracelets)

Aquamarine

To dream of aquamarine signifies the making of new friends; to wear aquamarine earrings brings love and affection. Aquamarine, a universal symbol of youth, hope, and health, blesses those born in March. (Before the fifteenth century it was considered to be the birthstone for those born in October.)

Aquamarine is a member of the important beryl family, which includes emerald, but aquamarine is less brittle and more durable than its green counterpart (7½ to 8 on Mohs' scale). Aquamarine ranges in color from light blue to bluish green to deep blue, the latter being the most valuable and desirable. It is a very wearable gem, clear and brilliant, and unlike emerald is available with excellent clarity even in very large sizes, although these are becoming scarce today. Aquamarines are still widely available in sizes up to fifteen carats, but ten-carat sizes with fine color and clarity are becoming scarce and are more expensive. Long considered a beautiful and moderately priced gem, it is now entering the "expensive" classification for stones in larger sizes with a good deep blue color. The finest aquamarine is found in Brazil, but other important sources include Afghanistan, India, Madagascar, Nigeria, Pakistan, and Russia.

Several words of caution for those interested in this lovely gem. First, you may want to think twice before buying a pale or shallow-cut stone, since the color will become paler as dirt accumulates on the back. These stones need constant cleaning to keep them beautiful. Second, be careful not to mistake blue topaz for aquamarine. While topaz is an equally beautiful gem, it is usually much less expensive, since it is usually treated to obtain its desirable color. For those who can't afford an aquamarine, however, blue topaz is an excellent alternative as long as it is properly represented and priced. Finally, note that many aquamarine-colored synthetic spinels are erroneously sold as aquamarine.

USEFUL FACTS

Aquamarine Composition: beryllium aluminum silicate
Weight: light (specific gravity: 2.68–2.90)

Brilliance: moderate
Hardness: 7.5–8.0
Wearability: very good

Benitoite

This exquisitely beautiful and rare gem is seldom seen in jewelry but is very popular among collectors and connoisseurs. Discovered in San Benito, California—hence the name *benitoite*—this remains the only source of this gemstone. It was recently selected as the official state stone of California, and we are beginning to see more of it in fine jewelry houses there.

Benitoite ranges from colorless to dark blue (often with a violet tint) to violet. A rare pink variety has also been identified. Benitoite can display fire, the dispersion of white light into the rainbow colors, comparable to a diamond, and is also very brilliant. Some might easily mistake it at a glance for a blue diamond. It lacks diamond's incredible hardness, however, and is more comparable to amethyst in hardness (6½ on Mohs' scale). It is difficult to find benitoite in sizes over 1 carat; only about five stones per year are cut that weigh 2 carats or more; only one every five years yields a stone 5 carats or more. Benitoite's rarity keeps it very expensive—a fine 1-carat stone could easily cost $3,000—and 2-carat sizes with fine color are extremely rare and even more costly. The largest fine benitoite known weighs just over 7¾ carats and is on display at the Smithsonian Institution in Washington, D.C.

For jewelry, benitoite is a relatively wearable stone, but given its rarity and value, I recommend that it be set in a somewhat protective mounting so that it is not easily subjected to accidental scratching or wear.

USEFUL FACTS

Benitoite Composition: barium titanium silicate   **Hardness**: 6.5
Weight: heavy (specific gravity: 3.65–3.68)   **Wearability**: fair to good
Brilliance: high to very high

Beryl (Golden Beryl and Morganite)

As early as A.D. 1220, the virtues of beryl were well established in legend. Beryl provided help against foes in battle or litigation, made the wearer unconquerable but at the same time friendly and likable, and also sharpened the wearer's intellect and cured laziness. Today beryl is still considered important, but primarily for aesthetic reasons. The variety of colors in which it is found, its wonderful clarity (except for emerald), its brilliance, and its durability (7½ to 8 on Mohs' scale; again with the exception of emerald) have given the various varieties of beryl tremendous appeal.

Most people are familiar with the blue variety of beryl, aquamarine, and the green variety, emerald. Few as yet know the pink variety, morganite, and the beautiful yellow to yellow-green variety, referred to as golden beryl. These gems have only recently found their place in the jewelry world but are already being shown in fabulous pieces made by the greatest designers. While not inexpensive, they still offer excellent value and beauty. The finest golden beryl (also called Heliodor) is found in Russia and Madagascar, but it is also found in Brazil, Namibia, the United States, and Ukraine. Fine pink morganite is primarily found in Madagascar and Brazil, but it is also found in Italy, Mozambique, Namibia, Pakistan, the United States, and Zimbabwe.

Beryl has also been found in many other colors—lilac, salmon, orange, sea green—as well as colorless. While most of these varieties are not as yet available to any but the most ardent rock hound, the orange varieties are fairly common and can still be found for under $125 per carat. Some orange varieties are heated to produce the more popular pink color and then sold as morganite. The rarest color is red, which is even more rare than emerald and is comparable in cost. It is often called *red emerald* (see the *Emerald* section above).

USEFUL FACTS

Beryl Composition: beryllium aluminum silicate   **Hardness**: 7.5–8.0
Weight: light (specific gravity: 2.68–2.90)   **Wearability**: good to very
Brilliance: moderately high   good

Bloodstone (Heliotrope)

Believed by the ancient Greeks to have fallen from heaven, this stone has held a prominent place throughout history, and even into modern times, as a great curative. It was (and still is in some parts of the world) believed capable of stopping every type of bleeding, clearing bloodshot eyes, acting as an antidote for snakebite, and relieving urinary troubles. Today there are people who wear bloodstone amulets to prevent sunstroke and headache and to provide protection against the evil eye.

The birthstone for March, bloodstone is a more or less opaque, dark green variety of quartz with specks of red jasper (a variety of quartz) spattering red throughout the dark green field. Particularly popular for men's rings (perhaps they need more protection from illness?) bloodstone is most desirable when the green isn't so dark as to approach black and the red flecks are roundish and pronounced. It is moderately durable (7 on Mohs' scale), and is fairly readily available and inexpensive. India is the major source of bloodstone, but it is also found in Australia, Brazil, China, and the United States.

USEFUL FACTS

Bloodstone Composition: silicon dioxide   **Hardness**: 7.0
Weight: light (specific gravity: 2.61)   **Wearability**: good
Brilliance: NA

Chrysoberyl and Cat's-Eye

The chrysoberyl family is very interesting because all three of its varieties—alexandrite, cat's-eye, and chrysoberyl—while chemically alike, are quite distinct from one another in their optical characteristics and bear no visible resemblance to one another.

Chrysoberyl in its cat's-eye variety has long been used as a charm to guard against evil spirits. One can understand why, given the pronounced eye effect: the eye, so legend has it, could see all, and it watched out for its wearer. But it was also believed that to dream of cat's-eye signified treachery. On still another level, it symbolized long life for the wearer, perhaps as a result of being protected from the evil eye.

Cat's-eye chrysoberyl (8½ on Mohs' scale) is a hard, translucent gem ranging in color from a honey yellow or honey brown to yellowish green to an almost emerald green. It has a velvety or silklike texture and, when properly cut, displays a brilliant whitish line of light right down the center, appearing almost to be lighted from inside. Genuine cat's-eye should not be confused with the common quartz variety, which is often yellow-brown (tiger's-eye) or bluish (hawk's-eye). The quartz variety has a much less striking eye and weaker color altogether. This phenomenon is produced only in cabochons.

To see the effect properly, the stone should be viewed under a single strong light source, coming if possible from directly overhead. If the line is not exactly in the center, the stone's value is reduced. The line does shift from side to side when the stone is moved about—probably another reason ancient people believed it capable of seeing all and guarding its wearer.

The stone called chrysoberyl, on the other hand, is a brilliant, transparent, very clear, and very durable stone (8½ on Mohs' scale) found in yellow, yellow-green, and green varieties. The finest chrysoberyl comes from Russia, but Sri Lanka is also an important source. It is also found in Brazil, Madagascar, Myanmar, Tanzania, and Zimbabwe. Cat's-eye is found in Brazil, China, and Sri Lanka.

This is another stone that still offers excellent value. It's a real beauty, very moderately priced, and just beginning to be appreciated and used in contemporary jewelry.

USEFUL FACTS
Chrysoberyl Composition: beryllium aluminum oxide   **Hardness**: 8.5
Weight: heavy (specific gravity: 3.71–3.72)   **Wearability**: excellent
Brilliance: NA

Chrysocolla

(See *Quartz*—true chrysocolla is a very soft copper-related mineral too soft for jewelry use.)

Chrysoprase and Carnelian

Chrysoprase has long been the subject of marvelous stories. In the 1800s, it was believed that a thief sentenced to be hanged or beheaded would immediately escape if he placed a chrysoprase in his mouth. Of course, it might be hard to obtain the stone unless he just happened to carry one around! And Alexander the Great was believed to have worn a "prase" in his girdle during battle, to ensure victory.

Chrysoprase is an inexpensive, highly translucent, bright, light green to dark green variety of quartz. While its color is often very uniform and can be very lovely in jewelry, for many years these gems have been dyed to enhance their color, where necessary. Chrysoprase is another stone that is usually cut in cabochon style. It has become very popular for jewelry as a fashion accessory. Do not confuse it with jade, however. It is sometimes called Australian jade and is sometimes misrepresented as real jade.

If you're the timid sort, carnelian is the stone for you. "The wearing of carnelians is recommended to those who have a weak voice or are timid in speech, for the warm-colored stone will give them the courage they lack so that they will speak both boldly and well," reports G. F. Kunz, a turn-of-the-century gemologist and historian.

This stone is especially revered by Moslems, because Muhammad himself wore a silver ring set with a carnelian engraved for use as a seal.

Napoleon I, while on a campaign in Egypt, picked up with his own hands (apparently from the battlefield) an unusual octagonal carnelian upon which was engraved the legend "The Slave Abraham Relying upon the Merciful [God]." He wore it with him always and bequeathed it to his nephew.

Carnelian, one of the accepted birthstones for August, is a reddish orange to brownish orange variety of quartz. A moderately hard (7 on Mohs' scale), translucent to opaque stone, its warm uniform color and fair durability have made it a favorite. It is often found in antique jewelry and lends itself to engraving or carving, especially in cameos. Today the best chrysoprase is found in Australia, but it is also found in Austria, Brazil, the Czech Republic, Poland, Russia, and the United States. The major source of carnelian is India. It is still a relatively inexpensive stone with great warmth and beauty and offers an excellent choice for jewelry to be worn as an accessory with today's fashion colors.

USEFUL FACTS

Chrysoprase and Carnelian Composition: silicon dioxide
Weight: light (specific gravity: 2.60–2.65)

Brilliance: NA
Hardness: 7.0
Wearability: Good

Citrine

(See *Quartz.*)

Coral

Coral, which for twenty centuries or more was classed with precious gems and can be found adorning ancient amulets alongside diamond, ruby, emerald, and pearl, had been "experimentally proved" by the sixteenth century to cure madness, give wisdom, stop the flow of blood from

beautifully carved jade is actually serpentine, which can be scratched easily with a knife.

Soapstone may also look like jade to the amateur, especially when beautifully carved. This stone is so soft that it can easily be scratched with a pin, hairpin, or point of a pen. It is much less expensive than comparable varieties of jade, as well as softer and less durable.

Jade is a wonderful stone, and imperial jade is breathtaking; no wonder it was the emperor's stone! But jade has long been "copied"—misrepresented and altered. Just be sure you know you are buying what you think you are buying.

Labradorite, Sunstone, and Spectrolite (Feldspar)

Labradorite is a fascinating stone that is starting to appear in some of the more distinctive jewelry salons, especially in beads and carved pieces, and is a member of the feldspar family (6 to 6½ on Mohs' scale). The most frequently seen variety is a grayish, almost opaque stone, within which startlingly brilliant flashes of peacock blue, greens, and/or yellows are visible at certain angles.

A beautiful, shimmering red to orange variety (and occasionally green or bicolor) known as *sunstone* is also beginning to enter the jewelry scene. Mined in Oregon, this wonderful, truly American gem is being featured in major United States retailers such as Tiffany. Finland also produces a very lovely variety of labradorite, often called spectrolite, that occurs in colors resembling peacock hues or the colors seen on the wings of butterflies. It can also exhibit a cat's-eye effect.

Labradorite is usually cut in cabochon style, but sunstone also occurs in a transparent material that makes a beautiful faceted gem. There are some glass imitations, but they don't come close to the real thing. This is a stone that is still relatively inexpensive and one to consider seriously if you want something striking and unusual.

USEFUL FACTS

Feldspar Composition: sodium calcium aluminosilicate
Weight: light (specific gravity: 2.68–2.70)
Brilliance: moderately brilliant; highly iridescent

Hardness: 6.0–6.5
Wearability: good ("tougher" than some harder gems)

Lapis Lazuli

Lapis, a birthstone for December, has been highly prized since ancient Babylonian and Egyptian times. An amulet of "great power" was formed when lapis was worked into the form of an eye and ornamented with gold—in fact, so powerful that sometimes these eyes were put to rest on the limbs of a mummy. In addition, it was recognized as a symbol for capacity, ability, success, and divine favor.

Genuine lapis is a natural blue opaque stone of intense, brilliant, deep blue color. It sometimes possesses small, sparkling gold-colored or silver-colored flecks (pyrite inclusions), although the finest quality is a deep, even blue with a purplish tint or undertone and no trace of those flecks. Occasionally it may be blue mottled with white. The finest lapis comes from Afghanistan and Argentina, but other sources include Russia, Chile, and Canada. Occasionally it is found in the United States.

Don't confuse genuine lapis with the cheaper "Swiss lapis" or "Italian lapis," which aren't lapis at all. These are natural stones (usually quartz) artificially colored to look like lapis lazuli. Genuine lapis is often represented as "Russian lapis," although it doesn't always come from Russia. The finest lapis comes from Afghanistan.

Lapis has become very fashionable, and the finest-quality lapis is becoming more rare and more expensive. This has resulted in an abundance of lapis that has been "color improved." It is often fashioned today with other gems—pearls, crystal, coral—that make particularly striking fashion accessories.

Sodalite is sometimes confused with the more expensive, and rarer, lapis and is used as a substitute for it. However, sodalite rarely contains the silvery or golden flecks typical of most lapis. It may have some white veining, but more commonly it just exhibits the fine lapis blue without any markings. The lapis substitutes transmit some light through the edges of the stone; lapis does not, since it is opaque.

USEFUL FACTS

Lapis Lazuli Composition: rock containing lazuli and other minerals
Weight: light (specific gravity: 2.6–2.7)

Brilliance: NA
Hardness: 5.5
Wearability: fair to good

Dyed chalcedony (quartz), glass, and plastic imitations are common. One quick and easy test to identify genuine lapis is to put a drop of hydrochloric acid on the stones; this will immediately produce the odor of a rotten egg. This test should be administered only by a professional, however, since hydrochloric acid can be dangerous.

Malachite and Azurite

Malachite must have been the answer to a mother's prayer. According to legend, attaching malachite to the neck of a child would ease its pain when cutting teeth. Also, tied over a woman in labor, it would ensure an easier, faster birth. It could also cure diseases of the eye. More important, however, it was believed capable of protecting from the evil eye and bringing good luck.

Malachite is also popular today, but perhaps more because of the exquisite color and a softness (3½ on Mohs' scale) that makes it very popular for carving. Malachite is a copper ore that comes in a brilliant kelly green, marked with bands or concentric striping in contrasting shades of the same basic green. It is opaque and takes a good polish, but it is soft and should not be worn in rings. This softness, however, makes it a favorite substance for use in carved bases, boxes, beads, statues, spheres, and so on. It is also used in pins, pendants, and necklaces (usually of malachite beads). Malachite is often found in copper-producing areas. Russia was once a major source, but today Zaire is the major producer.

Azurite is also a copper ore, but it occurs in a very vivid deep blue, similarly marked. Occasionally one will come across both azurite and malachite intermingled in brilliant combinations of color and striking patterns. In Israel, "Eilat stone" is usually azurite and malachite together, although it can also contain chrysocolla.

A particular note of caution: Never clean malachite or azurite with any product containing ammonia. In seconds the ammonia will remove all the polish, which will significantly reduce the stone's beauty.

USEFUL FACTS

Malachite Composition: copper hydroxycarbonate   **Hardness**: 3.5 (soft)
Weight: heavy (specific gravity: 3.80)   **Wearability**: fair to poor
Brilliance: NA

Azurite Composition: copper hydroxycarbonate   **Hardness**: 4.0 (soft)
Weight: heavy (specific gravity: 3.77)   **Wearability**: fair
Brilliance: NA

Moonstone (Orthoclase Feldspar)

Moonstone is definitely a good-luck stone, especially for lovers. As a gift the moonstone holds a high rank, for it is believed to arouse one's tender passion and to give lovers the ability to foretell their future—good or ill. To get this information, however, legend has it that the stone must be placed in the mouth while the moon is full. Perhaps a more important use, however, was in amulets made of moonstone, which would protect wearers from epilepsy and guarantee a greater fruit-crop yield when hung on fruit trees. The stone, in fact, assisted all vegetation.

The name *moonstone* is probably derived from the myth that one can observe the lunar month through the stone—that a small white spot appears in the stone as the new moon begins and gradually moves toward the stone's center, getting always larger, until the spot finally takes the shape of a full moon in the center of the stone.

Moonstone is a member of the feldspar family (6 to 6½ on Mohs' scale). It is a transparent, milky white to blue variety in which can be seen a floating white or blue light within the stone's body, an optical effect known as adularescence. It is a popular stone for rings because as the hand moves the adularescent effect is more pronounced. The bluer color is most desirable, but it is becoming rare in today's market, particularly in large sizes. The finest moonstone comes from Myanmar and Sri Lanka, but other sources include Brazil, India, Madagascar, Mexico, and Tanzania.

There are some glass imitations of moonstone, but compared with the real thing they are not very good.

USEFUL FACTS

Moonstone Composition: potassium aluminum silicate
Weight: light (specific gravity: 2.57)

Brilliance: NA
Hardness: 6–6.5
Wearability: good

Obsidian

Obsidian was widely used by the Mexicans, probably because of its brilliant polished surface, for making images of their god Tezcatlipoca and for polishing into mirrors used to divine the future. It has also been found in Egypt, fashioned into masks. It has been used since prehistoric times to make tools and weapons as well, such as arrowheads and other projectiles.

Obsidian is a semitranslucent to opaque glass that is smokey brown to black and sometimes a mixture of both. It is natural glass, not artificial. It is formed by volcanic activity and is also called volcanic glass. One variety, snowflake obsidian, exhibits white spots resembling snowflakes against or mingled with the black; some obsidian exhibits a strong iridescence; and some obsidian exhibits a sheen from within, as seen in moonstone.

Jewelry made from obsidian, which is available in great quantity and is very inexpensive, is a popular fashion accessory. It is particularly popular in Mexican and Native American jewelry and is seen fairly extensively in the West and in Mexico. Most obsidian jewelry today comes from North and Central America. One must exercise some caution, however, because obsidian is glass (5 on Mohs' scale) and can be scratched or cracked easily.

USEFUL FACTS
Obsidian Composition: primarily silicon dioxide   **Hardness:** 5.0
Weight: very light (specific gravity: 2.33–2.42)   **Wearability**: fair
Brilliance: moderately high

Onyx

Onyx is not a good-omen stone, and it is certainly not one for young lovers, since it is believed to bear an evil omen, to provoke discord and separate them. Worn around the neck, it was said to cool the ardors of love. The close union and yet strong contrast between the layers of black and white in some varieties may have suggested onyx's connection with romance. It was also believed to cause discord in general, create disharmony among friends, bring bad dreams and broken sleep to its wearer, and cause pregnant women to give birth prematurely.

But there isn't complete agreement as to its unlucky nature. Indians and Persians believe that wearing onyx will protect them from the evil eye, and that onyx placed on the stomach of a woman in labor will reduce the labor pain and bring on earlier delivery. So you choose—good or bad?

Onyx is a lovely, banded, semitranslucent to opaque quartz. It comes naturally in a variety of colors—reds, oranges, reddish orange, apricot, and shades of brown from cream to dark, often alternating with striking bands of white. The banding in onyx is straight, while curved bands occur in the variety of quartz known as agate. Onyx is used extensively for cameo and other carving work. It is also frequently dyed.

The "black onyx" that is commonly used in jewelry isn't onyx at all and isn't naturally black. It is chalcedony (another variety of quartz) dyed black. It is *always* dyed and may be banded or solid black.

Do not confuse the quartz variety of onyx with cave onyx, which is found in the stalactites and stalagmites of underground caves. Cave onyx is a different material altogether. It is much softer, lacks the color variety, and is much less expensive than quartz onyx.

USEFUL FACTS
Onyx Composition: silicon dioxide   **Hardness**: 7.0
Weight: light (specific gravity: 2.61)   **Wearability**: good
Brilliance: NA

Opal

The opal has suffered from an unfortunate reputation as being an evil stone and bearing an ill omen. Ominous superstitions surround this wonderful gem, including the belief that misfortune will fall on those who wear it. But its evil reputation has never been merited and probably resulted from a careless reading of Sir Walter Scott's poem *Anne of Geierstein,* in which the ill-fated heroine received an opal before her untimely death.

Among the ancients, opal was a symbol of fidelity and assurance, and in later history it became strongly associated with religious emotion and prayer. It was believed to have a strong therapeutic value for diseases of the eye, and worn as an amulet it would make the wearer immune from them as well as increase the powers of the eyes and the mind. Further, many believed that to the extent the colors of red and green (ruby and emerald) were seen, the wearer would also enjoy the therapeutic powers of those stones: the power to stop bleeding from the ruby or the power to cure kidney diseases from the emerald. The black opal was particularly highly prized as the luck stone of anyone lucky enough to own one!

This stone, whose brilliance and vibrant colors resemble the colors of the fall, is certainly appropriate as a birthstone for October. When we try to describe the opal, we realize how insufficient the English language is. It is unique among the gems, displaying an array of very brilliant miniature rainbow effects, all mixed together.

Its most outstanding characteristic is this unusual, intense display of many colors flashing out like mini-rainbows. This effect is created by opal's formation process, which is very different from that of other gems. Opal is composed of hydrated silica spheres. The mini-rainbows seen in most opals result from light interference created by these spheres. The arrangement of the spheres, which vary in size and pattern, is responsible for the different colors.

Opal is usually cut flat or in cabochon, since there is no additional brilliance to be captured by faceting. In opals, color is everything. The more brilliant the color, the more valuable the gem. It is probably truer of opal than any other stone that the more beautiful the stone and its color, the more it will cost. But it is fairly soft (5½ to 6½ on Mohs' scale), so opals should be treated with care.

Opal is generally categorized based upon the body color—*light* or *dark*—and the degree of transparency. By body color we don't mean the rainbow colors, but rather its base tone, which can be colorless or white, various gray shades, or black. "Light opal" includes all the shades through medium gray; "dark opal" includes dark gray to black.

Opal can exhibit varying degrees of transparency from opaque to translucent to transparent. When an opal is transparent or very translucent and the clarity of the color is very sharp, it is called *crystal*—the play of color must be visible both on the surface and within the stone. When the color in such a stone is hazy, we refer to the opal as a *jelly* opal. You may also hear the terms *semi-crystal* or *semi-jelly* or *water opals* used to describe opals with such transparency. *Fire* opal is a crystal or jelly opal with an intense, fiery red-orange color.

The type of opal that first comes to mind when most people think of opal is white opal, but connoisseurs seek black opals, the rarest of all. Black opals are usually a deep gray or grayish black with flashes of incredibly brilliant color dancing around within and about the stones as they are turned. One must be careful when purchasing a black opal, however, to ensure that it is not a doublet or triplet: a stone composed of two or three parts of some material fused or glued together. There are many such doublets on the market because of the black opal's rarity, beauty, and extremely high cost; a black opal the size of a lima bean could cost $25,000 today. The black opal doublet provides an affordable option to one who loves the stone but can't afford a natural. But it also provides another opportunity for misrepresentation that can be very costly to the consumer.

Generally speaking, purity of color, absence of dead spots (called trueness), flawlessness, intensity or brilliance of color, and transparency are the primary factors affecting value. Opals with an abundance of red are usually the most expensive, whether a light or dark opal; those strong in blue and green are equally beautiful but less rare, so their price is somewhat less. One of the rarest is the harlequin opal, which displays color patterns resembling a checker board, and these can be incredibly costly. Australia is the leading producer of all types of opal, but other sources include southern Africa, Brazil, Czech Republic, Mexico, and the United States.

While there are imitations and synthetics, for the most part their quality is such that they are not yet worth considering. The synthetic opal, nonetheless, is being used extensively. Also, since the color of black opals can be improved by treatment, treated opals are encountered frequently. So the usual precautions are in order: make sure you know what you are getting, and before buying, shop around. This holds truer for opal, perhaps, than any other stone.

One word of caution must also be offered: opals require special care because some tend to dry and crack. Avoid exposure to anything that is potentially drying, and immerse your opal in water for several hours periodically to help preserve it. *Never wipe the surface of opals with oil or immerse them in oil;* soaking some opals in oil for only a few hours can cause them to lose some or nearly all of their fire. Furthermore, it was once thought that wiping the surface of an opal regularly with oil would protect it. *This is not true and will damage most opals.*

USEFUL FACTS

Opal Composition: hydrated silica gel   **Hardness**: 5.5–6.5
Weight: very light (specific gravity: 1.98–2.20)   **Wearability**: fair to good
Brilliance: NA

Peridot (Olivine)

Today's birthstone for August, peridot was also a favorite of the ancients. This lovely transparent yellowish green to deep chartreuse stone was quite a powerful gem. It was considered an aid to friendship and was also believed to free the mind of envious thoughts (which is probably why it was an aid to friendship). Because of its yellowish green color, it was also believed to cure or prevent diseases of the liver and dropsy. If that's not enough, worn on the left arm it would protect the wearer from the evil eye.

Peridot is also popular today, but probably more for its lovely shade of green than its professed powers. While peridot is not particularly brilliant, the richness of its color can be exceptional and it is natural. Peridot is one of the few gems that is not routinely treated. It comes in shades of yellowish green to darker, purer green colors. Unfortunately, because of its rarity most people never see peridot in the deeper, purer green color that is so prized, but newly discovered sources may change this. Today sources of peridot include Arizona in the U.S., Mexico, Myanmar, Norway, Pakistan, Russian, and Sri Lanka.

Peridot is still widely available in small sizes, but larger stones are becoming scarce, so prices are now fairly high for good-quality material in higher carat weights.

Some caution should be exercised in wearing peridot. It is moderately hard (6½ to 7 on Mohs' scale) but can chip and scratch easily. Also, some stones—like green sapphire or green tourmaline—can look like peridot and be mistaken or misrepresented.

USEFUL FACTS

Peridot Composition: magnesium iron silicate
Weight: moderately heavy (specific gravity: 3.34)
Brilliance: moderate to high

Hardness: 6.5–7
Wearability: fair to good

Quartz

The most versatile of any of the gem families, quartz includes among its members more variety and a larger number of gems than any other three mineral families together. In the gem trade, the old saying "If in doubt, say quartz" still holds true.

The quartz minerals, for the most part, are relatively inexpensive gems that offer a wide range of pleasing color alternatives in both transparent and nontransparent varieties, from translucent to opaque. They are reasonably hard stones (7 on Mohs' scale) and, while not very brilliant in the transparent varieties, still create lovely, affordable jewelry.

Some of these gems have been discussed in separate sections, but I will provide a list here with brief descriptions of most of the quartz family members.

Transparent varieties. Amethyst (see page 110) is lilac to purple in color.

Citrine is often called quartz topaz, citrine topaz, or topaz, all of which are misleading. The correct name for this stone is citrine. It ranges in color from lemon yellow to egg-yolk yellow to an orangy amber or brownish amber color. This is the most commonly seen "topaz" in today's marketplace and is, unfortunately, too often confused with precious topaz because of the careless use of the name. While a pleasing stone in terms of color and fairly durable, citrine is slightly softer and has less brilliance than precious topaz. It also lacks the subtle color shading, the pinker yellow or pinkish amber shades, which lends to precious topaz a distinctive color difference. Much citrine is made by heating pale amethyst.

Citrine is much less expensive than precious topaz. It should never be represented as topaz, which technically is "precious" or "imperial" topaz. Unfortunately, it often is. For example, "topaz" birthstone jewelry is almost always citrine (or a worthless synthetic). So the question to ask the seller is, "Is this citrine or precious topaz?" Get the answer in writing if you are told, "Precious topaz."

Citrine is plentiful in all sizes and can be made into striking jewelry, especially in very large sizes, for a relatively small investment, while precious topaz of fine quality is scarce in sizes over seven carats and is *very* expensive.

Ametrine is a lovely, unusual bicolor quartz in which amethyst and citrine are both present in the same stone. The name is derived by taking the first three letters of amethyst and the last five letters in citrine. Bolivia is the source of natural ametrine, although "ametrine" can also be created in the laboratory.

Praseolite is a pale green transparent variety produced by heating amethyst.

Rock crystal is water clear. It was used in old jewelry for rondelles, a type of small bead resembling a doughnut. Faceted crystal beads were also common in older jewelry. Today, however, *crystal* usually refers to glass.

Rose quartz is light to deep pink. This stone has been very popular for many years for use in carved pieces—beads, statues, ashtrays, fine lamp bases, and pins and brooches. Rarely clear, this stone is usually seen in cabochon cuts, rounded beads, or carvings rather than in faceted styles. Once very inexpensive, it is becoming more costly, particularly in the finer deep pink shades. But the color of rose quartz is especially pleasing and offers an excellent choice for use in fashion accessory jewelry.

You must be somewhat cautious with rose quartz, however, because it tends to crack more easily than most other varieties of quartz if struck or exposed to a blow. The inclusions or internal fractures that are also responsible for the absence of clarity in this stone cause it to be slightly brittle.

Smokey quartz is a pale to rich smokey brown variety, sometimes mistaken for or misrepresented as smokey topaz or topaz. It is also very plentiful and is becoming popular for use in very large sizes for beautiful brooches, large dinner rings, and so forth.

Translucent to opaque varieties. **Agate** and *chalcedony* are found in all colors, and all varieties of markings are seen in this wonderful ornamental gem. Among them you'll find, to mention a few, banded agate; moss agate, a fascinating white or milky agate that looks as though it actually has black, brown, or green moss growing within; eye agate, which has an eyeball effect; or plume agate, which looks as if it's filled with beautiful feather plumes. The colors and "scenes" in agate are infinite. While agate is usually an inexpensive stone, some varieties or special stones with very unusual scenes or markings can be quite expensive.

Carnelian, sard, and *sardonyx* are reddish, orange, apricot, and brown varieties of chalcedony and are often seen in cameo or other carving work. Black onyx is a dyed chalcedony; chrysoprase is green chalcedony, often dyed green.

The unusual colors and markings of agate made it very highly regarded by the ancients and revered throughout history, even to the present day. According to Pliny, it was believed to make wearers "agreeable and persuasive and give them God's favor." Other virtues claimed for agate wearers include giving the wearer victory and strength and also protection from tempests and lightning, guarding its wearer from all dangers, enabling him to overcome all terrestrial obstacles, and imparting to him a bold heart.

Wearing agate ornaments was also seen as a cure for insomnia and could ensure good dreams. In the middle of the 1800s, and continuing to the present in some parts of the world, amulets made from eye agate (brown or black agate with a white ring in the center) were so popular that agate cutters in Germany had time for cutting little else. The "eye" was believed to take on the watchfulness of one's guardian spirit and to protect the wearer from the evil eye by neutralizing its power. At one time these amulets commanded an incredible price.

Whatever their real power, these are fascinating stones, some quite mesmerizing in their unusual beauty. They are often seen in antique jewelry as well as in contemporary pieces. One must be careful, however, to exercise some caution in wear to protect from knocks, as some varieties are more fragile than others. Also, agate is frequently dyed, so it is important to ask whether the color is natural and to be sure that it is not another less valuable stone, dyed to look like a special variety of agate.

Aventurine is a lovely pale to medium green semitranslucent stone with tiny sparkling flecks of mica within. This stone makes very lovely cabochon or bead jewelry at a very affordable price. It is occasionally misrepresented as jade; although the mica flecks are sometimes so small that they cannot be seen easily, they provide an immediate and reliable indicator that the material is aventurine quartz. Be aware, however, that there are some fairly good glass imitations in the marketplace.

Bloodstone (see page 116) is dark green with red spots.

Cat's-eye is a pale yellowish green stone that when cut in cabochon style produces a streak of light down the center that creates an eye effect. This phenomenon is a result of the presence of fiberlike inclusions. This stone has a weaker center line, a paler color, and much lower cost than true cat's-eye from the chrysoberyl family. But it is nonetheless an attractive stone that makes attractive, affordable jewelry.

Chrysocolla—the true chrysocolla— is a very soft copper mineral, too soft for jewelry use. However, quartz that has been naturally impregnated or stained with chrysocolla has good hardness and the same brilliant blue-green, highly translucent color. Chrysocolla is becoming a very popular stone for jewelry, and its price is starting to reflect increased demand.

Chrysoprase (see page 118) is a bright light to dark green, highly translucent stone, often of very even color. It is sometimes misrepresented as or confused with jade.

Jasper is opaque red, yellow, green, and brown (or sometimes gray). It is usually strongly marked in terms of the contrast between the green and other colors in an almost blotchlike or veinlike pattern. The red and green combination is the most popular, although there are more than fifty types of jasper of various colors and patterns.

Jasper was believed in ancient cultures to bring rain and also to protect its wearer from the bites of poisonous creatures. It was believed to have as diverse a power as the colors and veins in which it came, so many uses and magical powers were associated with it.

Jasper offers interesting color contrast and variety and is being used increasingly in today's fashion accessory jewelry.

Petrified wood is sections of trees or limbs that have been replaced by quartz-type silica and transformed into a mineral after centuries of immersion in silica-rich water under extreme pressure. It is usually red, reddish brown, or brown and is not often seen in jewelry.

Tiger's-eye is a golden, yellowish, reddish, and sometimes bluish variety of quartz that produces a bright shimmering line (or lines) of light, which when cut in a cabochon will produce an eye. The eye will move when the stone is turned from side to side. It is inexpensive but very popular for fashion accessory jewelry and men's cufflinks and rings. The blue variety is often called *hawk's-eye*.

USEFUL FACTS

Quartz Composition: silicon dioxide   **Hardness:** 7.0
Weight: light (specific gravity: 2.61–2.65)   **Wearability:** good
Brilliance: moderately high

Rhodochrosite

Rhodochrosite is a newcomer to the jewelry business. While sought by rock hounds for many years and a favorite of beginning lapidaries, rhodochrosite appeared only occasionally outside of rock and mineral shows frequented by hobbyists. A member of the carbonate mineral group, rhodochrosite is a relatively soft stone occurring in both a rare transparent and a more common nontransparent variety. For practical purposes, I will discuss the latter, more readily available form.

A lovely red to almost white color, often with agatelike curved lines creating a design in contrasting shades of red or pink, rhodochrosite may occasionally occur in an orangy tone, but this is poorer-quality material. The finest color is a medium to deep rose, preferably with curved banding. It has long been popular for certain ornamental objects (spheres, boxes, eggs) but only recently for jewelry. Today, necklaces using rhodochrosite beads alternating with other stones or gold beads are becoming particularly popular. We will see more rhodochrosite on the market in coming years, but it is soft (4 on Mohs' scale) so care should be used when wearing it to avoid unnecessary abuse. The major source of this variety of rhodochrosite is the United States.

USEFUL FACTS

Rhodochrosite Composition: manganese carbonate   **Hardness**: 4.0 (soft)
Weight: very heavy (specific gravity: 5.20)   **Wearability**: fair to good
Brilliance: NA

Scapolite

This is an interesting gem that is beginning to appear in more jewelry as it becomes more available. Found in Madagascar, Myanmar, and Canada, it was rediscovered in Brazil and also recently discovered in Kenya. Scapolite is a nice, transparent, fairly durable stone (6 on Mohs' scale) occurring in a range of colors, from colorless to yellow, light red, orange, greenish, bluish gray, violet, and violet-blue. The orange, light red, and whitish specimens may also occur as semitransparent stones, which may show a cat's-eye effect (chatoyancy) when cut into cabochons.

The most likely to appear in jewelry are the violets and yellows, and

---

USEFUL FACTS

Scapolite Composition: complex silicate   **Hardness**: 6.0
Weight: light (specific gravity: 2.70)   **Wearability**: fair
Brilliance: moderate

---

possibly orange cat's-eyes. They might easily be mistaken for yellow beryl or certain quartz minerals like amethyst or citrine.

The bottom line here is that we will have to wait and see what trends evolve around this stone, as its availability will determine its future use and cost.

Serpentine

Serpentine derives its name from its similarity to the green speckled skin of the serpent. Amulets of serpentine were worn for protection from serpent bites, stings of poisonous reptiles, and poison in general. A king was reputed to have insisted that his chalice be made of serpentine, as it was believed that if a poisoned drink were put into a serpentine vessel, the vessel would sweat on the outside. The effectiveness of medicine was increased when it was drunk from a serpentine vessel.

Serpentine is often used as a jade substitute. It is a translucent to semi-translucent stone occurring in light to dark yellowish green to greenish yellow. One variety is used for decorative wall facings and table and counter surfaces, but some of the more attractive green varieties so closely resemble jadeite or nephrite jade that they are used in carvings and jewelry and are often misrepresented as jade. Common serpentine is also sometimes dyed a jadelike color. One lovely green variety, williamsite, which is a very pleasing deep green, often with small black flecks within, is often sold as "Pennsylvania jade." It is pretty, but it is not jade. Another variety of serpentine, bowenite, is also sold today as "Korean jade" or "new jade." Again, it is pretty but is not jade. Serpentine is softer than jade, less durable, and much more common, which its price should reflect. Sources of serpentine include Afghanistan, China, England, Italy, New Zealand, South Africa, and the United States.

It is a lovely stone in its own right and makes a nice alternative to jade. While it has been around for a long time (too often, however, represented as jade), we are just beginning to see this stone used frequently in necklaces and other fine jewelry under its own name.

USEFUL FACTS

Serpentine Composition: magnesium hydroxysilicate   **Hardness**: 5.0
Weight: light (specific gravity: 2.58–2.62)   **Wearability**: fair to good
Brilliance: moderate

Sodalite

This stone has already been discussed under *Lapis*. It is a dark blue semitransparent to semitranslucent stone, used frequently as a substitute for the rarer, more expensive lapis. While it may have some white veining, it does not have the golden or silver flecks that are characteristic of lapis. If you do not see these shiny flecks, suspect that the stone is probably sodalite. The major commercial source of sodalite is Ontario, Canada. It is sometimes called *Princess Blue* since it was discovered there during a visit by Princess Margaret. Other sources include Brazil, India, Namibia, and the United States.

USEFUL FACTS

Sodalite Composition: sodium aluminum silicate   **Hardness:** 5.5
Weight: light (specific gravity: 2.27)   **Wearability:** fair to good
Brilliance: NA

Spinel

Spinel is one of the loveliest of the gems, but it has only recently begun to enjoy the respect and admiration it deserves. It is usually compared to sapphire or ruby rather than being recognized for its own intrinsic beauty and value. There is also a common belief that spinel (and similarly zircon) is synthetic rather than natural, when in fact it is one of nature's most beautiful—and truly natural—creations. This misconception probably arose because synthetic spinel is seen frequently on the market, whereas genuine spinel is not often seen.

Spinel is one of the very few gems currently *not enhanced or treated*. It occurs in red-orange (flame spinel), light to dark orangy red, light to dark slightly grayish blue, greenish blue, grayish green, and dark to light purple to violet. It also occurs in yellow and in an opaque variety—black. When compared with the blue of sapphire or the red of ruby, the color is usually considered less intense (although some red spinel can look very much like some ruby on the market now), yet its brilliance can be greater. If you appreciate these spinel colors for themselves, they are quite pleasing. The most popular are red (usually a more orange-red than ruby red) and blue (sometimes resembling a strong Bromo-Seltzer–bottle blue).

One of the most famous of all stones—the "Black Prince's Ruby" that adorns the famous Imperial State Crown, part of the British crown jewels—was discovered to be a red spinel! Throughout history, natural spinel has been confused and misidentified as many other gemstones—some less valuable, some more valuable—including ruby, sapphire, zircon, amethyst, garnet, synthetic ruby/sapphire, and even glass. Then, to make matters more complex, synthetic spinel is used to make composite stones such as emerald doublets.

Spinel is a hard (8 on Mohs' scale), fairly durable stone with good brilliance and a lively personality. It occurs in many lovely colors and still offers very good value. The primary sources of spinel are Madagascar, Myanmar, and Sri Lanka, but others include Afghanistan, Australia, Brazil, Italy, Pakistan, Russia, Sweden, Turkey, and the United States.

As more and more people discover this lovely gemstone, however, prices may increase significantly. We are already seeing prices strengthen.

USEFUL FACTS
Spinel Composition: magnesium aluminum oxide   **Hardness**: 8.0
Weight: heavy (specific gravity: 3.60)   **Wearability**: good to very
Brilliance: high   good

Sphene

(See *Titanite*.)

Spodumene (Kunzite and Hiddenite)

Spodumene is another gem relatively new to widespread jewelry use. The most popular varieties are kunzite and hiddenite. Kunzite was named after the famous American gemologist, George Frederick Kunz, and hiddenite was named after an American gemologist, William Hidden, who discovered the green variety in North Carolina, in the area that now also bears his name, Hiddenite.

Kunzite is a very lovely brilliant stone occurring in delicate lilac, pinkish, or violet shades. Its color can fade in strong light, so it has become known as an "evening" stone. Also, while a relatively hard stone (6 to 7 on Mohs' scale), it is nonetheless brittle and can break easily if it receives a sharp blow from certain directions. It is not recommended for rings for this reason unless set in a protective mounting. But it is a lovely gem, whose low cost makes it attractive in large sizes, and is an excellent choice for lovely, dramatic jewelry design.

Hiddenite is rarer. Light green or yellow-green varieties are available, but the emerald green varieties are scarce. As with kunzite, it is relatively hard but brittle, so you must be careful when wearing it.

Spodumene also occurs in many other shades of color, all pale but very clear and brilliant. Only blue is currently missing—but who knows what may yet be discovered in some part of the world? Primary sources of kunzite and hiddenite are Brazil, Madagascar, Myanmar, and Pakistan, but they are also found in Canada, Mexico, Russia, Sweden, and the United States.

Spodumene is still fairly inexpensive and is an excellent choice for contemporary jewelry design. Be careful, however, as it can be confused with and sold as more expensive topaz, tourmaline, spinel, or beryl. Also, synthetic corundum or spinel can be mistaken for this gem.

USEFUL FACTS

Spodumene Composition: lithium aluminum silicate   **Hardness**: 6–7.0
Weight: moderately heavy (specific gravity: 3.18)   **Wearability**: fair to good
Brilliance: high

Sugilite

Named for the Japanese petrologist who discovered it, Ken-ichi Sugi, sugilite first appeared on the jewelry scene in the late 1970s, sold as Royal Azel and Royal Lavulite. Best known today as sugilite, its lovely, deep rich purple to purple-red color is unique. An opaque gem, it is usually cut in cabochons or beads, although it is also popular for inlay work (intarsia) by top artisans. Sugilite belongs to the manganese family, and most comes from Africa. The finest color is already becoming scarce, so it is difficult to predict the future for this interesting newcomer.

USEFUL FACTS

Sugilite Composition: sodium/lithium silicate   **Hardness**: 6.0–6.5
Weight: slightly heavy (specific gravity: 2.74–2.80)   **Wearability**: fair to good
Brilliance: moderate

Tanzanite

(See *Zoisite*.)

Titanite (Sphene)

This is another "new" gem that is beginning to appear and offers some interesting possibilities for the jewelry market. While it has been highly regarded for many years, its relative scarcity prevented its widescale use in jewelry. Today, however, new sources have been discovered, and we are beginning to see greater availability. Today titanite is found primarily in Brazil and Madagascar, but it can also be found in Austria, Canada, Mexico, and Switzerland.

This is a beautiful, brilliant stone, with a diamondlike (adamantine) luster, and fire that is even greater than in diamond. Unfortunately, it is soft. Its colors range from grass green to golden yellow to brown.

There is need for some caution because of this stone's softness (5 to 5½ on Mohs' scale). I suggest that it is especially suitable for pendants, earrings, brooches, and protective ring settings.

USEFUL FACTS

Titanite Composition: calcium titanium silicate **Hardness**: 5.0–5.5 (soft)
Weight: heavy (specific gravity: 3.53) **Wearability**: fair
Brilliance: very high

Topaz

True topaz, symbol of love and affection, aid to sweetness of disposition, and birthstone for November, is one of nature's most wonderful and least-known families. The true topaz is rarely seen in jewelry stores. Unfortunately, most people know only the quartz (citrine) topaz, or glass, and in the past almost any yellow stone was called topaz. A very beautiful and versatile stone, topaz is a hard, brilliant stone with a fine color range, and it is much rarer and much more expensive than the stones commonly sold as topaz. It is also heavier than its imitators.

Topaz occurs not only in the transparent yellow, yellow-brown, orangy brown, and pinky brown colors most popularly associated with it, but also in a very light to medium red now found naturally in fair supply, although many are produced through heat treatment. It also is found in a very light to medium deep blue, also often as the result of treatment, although blue does occur naturally on a fairly wide scale. Other topaz shades include very light green, light greenish yellow, violet, and colorless. Diffusion-treated topaz is also available in medium to deep green and blue-green.

Blue topaz has become very popular in recent years, most of it treated; unfortunately, there is no way yet to determine which have been treated and which are natural. The blue form closely resembles the finest aquamarine, which is very expensive today, and offers a very attractive and much more affordable alternative to it. Some of the fine, deeper blue treated topazes have been found to be radioactive and, according to the Nuclear Regulatory Commission, may be injurious to the wearer. In the United States, all blue topaz must be tested for radiation levels; the Gemological Institute of America (GIA) now provides this service to the jewelry trade. However, be very careful when buying blue topaz outside the United States. If you do, you may be wise to have it tested when you get home.

There are many misleading names to suggest that a stone is topaz when it is not, for example, "Rio topaz," "Madeira topaz," "Spanish topaz," and "Palmeira topaz." They are types of citrine (quartz) and should be represented as such.

The true topaz family offers a variety of color options in lovely, clear, brilliant, and durable stones (8 on Mohs' scale). Precious topaz can be found in Africa, Australia, Brazil, Japan, Mexico, Myanmar, Pakistan, Russia, Sri Lanka, and Tasmania. The major sources of pink topaz are Brazil, Pakistan, and Russia. This family should become more important in the years ahead.

USEFUL FACTS

Topaz Composition: aluminum fluorohydroxysilicate   **Hardness**: 8.0
Weight: heavy (specific gravity: 3.54)   **Wearability**: good
Brilliance: high

Tourmaline

Tourmaline is a gem of modern times, but nonetheless it has found its way to the list of birthstones, becoming an "alternative birthstone" for October. Perhaps this honor results from tourmaline's versatility and broad color range, or perhaps from the fact that red and green tourmaline, in which red and green occur side by side in the same stone, is reminiscent of the turning of October leaves.

Whatever the case, tourmaline is one of the most versatile of the gem families. It is available in every color, in every tone from deep to pastel, and even with two or more colors appearing in the same stone side by side. There are bicolored tourmalines (half red and half green, for example) and tricolored (one-third blue, one-third green, and one-third yet another color). The fascinating "watermelon" tourmaline looks just like the inside of a watermelon: red in the center surrounded by a green "rind." A rare new "particolor" variety (more than three colors) called Liddicoatite—named to honor American gemologist Richard Liddicoat—was discovered in Brazil and Madagascar. It is marked by multiple-color banding and a three-rayed star that resembles the Mercedes logo. Tourmaline can also be found in a cat's-eye variety.

One of the most exciting gemological discoveries of this century was the discovery of a unique variety of tourmaline in Paraiba, Brazil. These particular beauties, referred to as Paraiba or Hetorita after the man who discovered them, have colors so intense and come in such a wide range of green, blue, and lilac shades that they are referred to as the *neon* tourmalines. Unfortunately, demand has been unprecedented for these particular tourmalines, and supply has dwindled. The result is that many of the finest Paraibas are very expensive, and some rival the finest sapphires and emeralds in price. Many imitations are now on the market, and I have found apatite, a common, inexpensive stone that occurs in similar colors but is too soft for most jewelry use, being sold as "Paraiba" tourmaline.

It is indeed surprising that most people know of tourmaline simply as a common "green" stone. Nothing could be more misleading. Today, we are finally beginning to see other lovely varieties of this fascinating gem in the jewelry market. In addition to the exciting new Paraiba, other popular varieties include the following:

- Chrome—a particularly rare green hue
- Indicolite—deep indigo blue, usually with a green undertone
- Rubellite—deep pink to red, as in ruby

While many tourmalines are very inexpensive, the chrome, indicolite, and rubellite varieties are priced (depending on size and quality) anywhere from $300 to $1,000 per carat or more. And the incomparable Paraiba varieties can sell for $2,000 to $4,000 per carat for a top quality one-carat stone—up to $15,000 *per carat* for a five-carat stone, if you can find one. So much for the "common and inexpensive" myth!

Tourmaline is a fairly hard (7 to 7½ on Mohs' scale), durable, brilliant, and very wearable stone with a wide range of colors. Tourmalines can be found in Australia, Brazil, East Africa, Nigeria, Madagascar, Mexico, Myanmar, Pakistan, Russia, South Africa, Sri Lanka, Tanzania, and the United States (California and Maine are important sources of fine tourmaline).

Tourmaline is a stone that will, without question, play a more and more important role in jewelry in the years ahead.

USEFUL FACTS

Tourmaline Composition: complex borosilicate
Weight: moderately heavy (specific gravity: 3.06)
Brilliance: NA

Hardness: 7–7.5
Wearability: good to excellent

Turquoise

A birthstone for December, and ranking highest among all the opaque stones, turquoise—the "Turkish stone"—is highly prized throughout Asia and Africa, not only for its particular hue of blue (a beautiful robin's-egg or sky blue) but especially for its supposed prophylactic and therapeutic qualities. The Arabs consider it a lucky stone and have great confidence in its benevolent action. Used in rings, earrings, necklaces, head ornaments, and amulets, it protects the wearer from poison, reptile bites, eye diseases, and the evil eye. It was also believed capable of warning of impending death by changing color. Also, the drinking of water in which turquoise has been dipped or washed was believed to cure bladder ailments. Buddhists revere the turquoise because it is associated with a legend in which a turquoise enabled Buddha to destroy a monster. Even today it is considered a symbol of courage, success, and love. It has also long been associated with Native American jewelry and art.

Turquoise is an opaque, light to dark blue or blue-green stone. The finest color is an intense blue, with poorer qualities tending toward yellowish green. The famous Persian (Iranian) turquoise, which can be a very intense and pleasing sky blue to robin's-egg blue, is a very rare and valuable gem. In Tibet there is a greener variety, which is preferred there. The United States (Arizona and New Mexico) is an important source of fine turquoise, some of which is comparable to the highly prized sky and robin's-egg blue associated with Iranian turquoise. Mexico continues to produce turquoise, although it is typically greener. Turquoise is also found in Australia, Chile, China, Russia, and Turkestan.

All turquoise is susceptible to aging, turning greenish or possibly darker over time. Also, care must be taken to avoid contact with soap, grease, or other materials that might discolor it and to protect it from abuse, since turquoise scratches fairly easily (6 on Mohs' scale).

But exercise caution when buying turquoise. This is a frequently simulated gem. Very fine glass imitations are produced that are difficult to distinguish from the genuine. Enhanced, coated, and "stabilized" stones, and reconstructed stones (from turquoise powder bonded in plastic), saturate the marketplace, as does synthetic turquoise. There are techniques to quickly distinguish these imitations and treated stones, so, if in doubt, check it out (and get a complete description on the bill of sale: "genuine, natural turquoise").

USEFUL FACTS

Turquoise Composition: hydrated copper aluminum phosphate
Weight: light (specific gravity: 2.80)

Brilliance: NA
Hardness: 6.0
Wearability: fair to good

Zircon

Known to the ancients as hyacinth, this gem had many powers, especially for men. While it was known to assist women in childbirth, for men it kept evil spirits and bad dreams away, gave protection against "fascination" and lightning, strengthened their bodies, fortified their hearts, restored appetite, suppressed fat, produced sleep, and banished grief and sadness from the mind.

Zircons are very brilliant, transparent stones that occur in several lovely colors. Unfortunately, many consumers suffer from a strange misconception that zircon is a synthetic or artificial stone rather than a lovely natural creation. Perhaps this is based on the fact that relatively inexpensive brown stones are routinely heated to transform them into colorless and blue. Despite the number of treated zircons in the market, they also occur naturally in a range of colors, including yellow, orange, red, green, and brown. Sri Lanka has been a source of gem-quality zircon for hundreds of years. It is also found in Australia, Brazil, Cambodia, France, Myanmar, Thailand, Tanzania, and Vietnam.

Many might mistake the colorless zircon for diamond because of its strong brilliance, which, coupled with its very low cost, makes colorless zircon an interesting alternative to diamonds as a stone to offset or dress up colored stones. But care needs to be exercised because zircon is only moderately hard (6½ to 7½ on Mohs' scale), and it is brittle, so it will chip or abrade easily. For this reason, zircon is recommended for earrings, pendants, brooches, or rings with a protective setting.

USEFUL FACTS

Zircon Composition: zirconium silicate
Weight: very heavy (specific gravity: 4.69)
Brilliance: very high

Hardness: 6.5–7.5
Wearability: fair

Zoisite (Tanzanite)

Zoisite was not considered a gem material until 1967, when a beautiful rich, blue to purple-blue, transparent variety was found in Tanzania (hence the name). Today the primary sources of tanzanite are Tanzania and Kenya. Tanzanite can occur naturally in a rich, sapphire blue color, possibly with some violet-red or greenish yellow flashes, but most have been heated to obtain the lovely blue and violet colors we see. A gem green variety has recently been discovered, which is being called green zoisite, green tanzanite, or chrome tanzanite. The green can be a very lovely shade, ranging from a slightly yellowish green to gray-green to bluish green, and the color is *natural*. The green variety is one of the few gems *not routinely treated*. Supply is still limited, so time will tell whether or not this green variety will be readily available to the public.

Tanzanite has become one of the most popular gems in the marketplace. As a result, many imitations are being produced. Double-check on the identity of any fine tanzanite with a gemologist-appraiser.

This lovely gem can cost over $2,000 per carat today in larger sizes.

But one must exercise care when wearing this stone because, while moderately hard (6½ on Mohs' scale), it is brittle and can chip easily. For this reason, I don't recommend it for rings (unless the ring provides some protection for the stones) or for everyday wear in which it would be exposed to knocks and other abuse. The green variety is somewhat more durable since it is not heated (heating can increase brittleness).

USEFUL FACTS

Tanzanite Composition: calcium aluminum hydroxysilicate

Weight: moderately heavy (specific gravity: 3.35)

Brilliance: high

Hardness: 6.5

Wearability: blue: fair; green: good

PART  THREE

Important Advice
Before & After You Buy

CHAPTER NINE

What to Ask When Buying the Stone

Asking the right questions is the key to knowing what you're getting when it comes to buying gemstones. It is also the only way you can be sure what you are comparing when considering gems from different jewelers. Be sure the jeweler can answer your questions or can get the answers for you. Then, be sure the jeweler is willing to put the answers *in writing* on your bill of sale. Finally, verify the facts—double-check that the stone is as represented—by having it examined by a qualified gemologist-appraiser. In this way you'll be able to make an informed choice about quality and value, you'll have no doubt about what you are getting, and you'll begin to develop a solid relationship with the jeweler from whom you make the purchase, based on confidence and trust. And, in the event the stone is not as represented, you'll know in time—and have the information you need—to get your money back.

What to Ask When Buying a Colored Gemstone

It is very important to ask the right questions to help you understand the differences in gems you may be considering. Asking the following questions should help you to gain a greater understanding of the differences, determine what's right for you, and have greater confidence in your decision.

1. *Is this a genuine, natural stone, or a synthetic?* Synthetic stones are *genuine* but not *natural* (see chapter 5).
2. *Is the color natural?* Most colored gemstones are routinely color enhanced (see chapters 5 and 6). However, stones such as lapis

should not be, and you must protect yourself from buying dyed material that will not retain its color permanently. See information on specific gems (chapters 7 and 8) to determine whether or not this is an important question for you to ask.

Be especially cautious when buying any blue sapphire; make sure you ask whether or not the stone has been checked for diffusion treatment and oiling. Today, with diffused sapphire being found mixed in parcels of natural sapphires and unknowingly set into jewelry, it's possible that one may be sold inadvertently (see chapter 6).

3. *Clarify what the name means.* Be particularly careful of misleading names (see chapter 6). When a stone is described with any qualifier, such as "Rio topaz" (which is not topaz), ask specifically whether or not the stone is genuine. Ask why the qualifier is being used.

4. *Is the clarity acceptable, or do too many inclusions detract from the beauty of the stone?* Are there any flaws, inclusions, or natural characteristics in this stone that might make it more vulnerable to breakage with normal wear? This is a particularly important question when you are considering a colored stone (see chapter 4). While visible inclusions are more common in colored gems than in diamonds, and their existence has much less impact on value than it has on diamond value, value is nonetheless reduced if the inclusions or blemishes affect the stone's durability, or are so numerous that they mar its beauty.

Be especially careful to ask whether or not any inclusion breaks the stone's surface, since this may weaken the stone, particularly if the imperfection is in a position normally exposed to wear, like the top of the stone or around the girdle. This would reduce the stone's value significantly. On the other hand, if the flaw is in a less vulnerable spot, where it can be protected by the setting, it may carry minimal risk and have little effect on value.

A large number of inclusions will usually detract noticeably from the beauty, especially in terms of liveliness, and will also generally weaken the stone and make it more susceptible to any blow or knock. Such stones should be avoided unless the price is right and you're willing to assume the risk.

Also, certain gems, as we've mentioned, are more brittle than others and may break or chip more easily, even without flaws.

These stones include opal, zircon, and some of the new and increasingly popular gems, such as tanzanite. This does not mean you should avoid buying them, but it does mean you should give thought to how they will be worn and how they will be set. Rings and bracelets are particularly vulnerable, since they are more susceptible to blows or knocks. Brooches, pendants, and earrings are less vulnerable.

5. *Do you like the color? How close is the color to its pure spectral shade? Is it too light? Too dark? How does the color look in different types of light?* Learn to look at color critically. Become familiar with the rarest and most valuable color of the gem of your choice. But after you do this, decide what you yourself really like. You may prefer a color that might be less rare and therefore more affordable. Be sure the color pleases you—don't buy what you think you *should* buy unless you really like it.

6. *Is the color permanent?* This question should be asked in light of new treatments (such as diffusion) and also because color in some stones is prone to fading. Two examples are amethyst and kunzite (one of the new and increasingly popular gems). Just which ones will fade and which ones won't, and how long the process might take, no one can know. This phenomenon has never affected the popularity of amethyst, and I see no reason for it to affect kunzite's popularity, but I feel the consumer should be aware of it. There is evidence that too much exposure to strong sunlight or intense heat contributes to fading in these stones, so I suggest avoiding sun and heat. It may be wise to wear these gems primarily for evening or indoor activities.

7. *Does the stone need a protective setting?* The setting may be of special importance when you are considering stones like tanzanite, opal, or emerald. They require a setting that will offer some protection—for example, one in which the main stone is surrounded by diamonds. A design in which the stone is unusually exposed, such as in a high setting or one with open, unprotected sides, would be undesirable.

8. *Does the stone have a pleasing shape? Does it have a nice "personality"?* This will be determined by the cutting. Many colored gems are cut in fancy shapes, often by custom cutters. Fine cutting can enrich the color and personality, and increase the cost. However, with colored gems, brilliance and sparkle are less important

than the color itself. The most critical considerations must focus on color, first and foremost. Sometimes a cutter must sacrifice brilliance in order to obtain the finest possible color. But if the color isn't rich enough or captivating enough to compensate for less brilliance, ask if the jeweler has something that is cut better and exhibits a little more sparkle. Keep in mind, however, that the more brilliant stone may not have the precise color you like, and that when you are buying a colored gem, *color* is the most crucial factor. Unless you find the stone's personality unappealing, don't sacrifice a beautiful color for a stone with a less appealing color just because it may sparkle more. Compare, and decide based on what you like and what you can afford.

When considering a pastel-colored gem, remember that if it is cut too shallow (flat), it can lose its appeal quickly (but only temporarily) with a slight buildup of greasy dirt on the back; the color will fade, and liveliness will practically disappear. This can be immediately remedied by a good cleaning.

9. *What are the colorless stones?* In a piece of jewelry where a colored stone is mounted with colorless stones to accentuate or highlight its color, ask, "What are the colorless stones?" Do not assume they are diamonds. They may be diamonds, zircons, artificial diamond imitations such as CZ or YAG, or synthetic white spinel (spinel is frequently used in Asia).

Special Tips to Remember When Buying a Colored Stone

When looking at unmounted stones, view them through the side as well as from the top. Also, turn them upside down on a flat white surface so they are resting on the table facet and you can look straight down through the stone from the back. Look for evenness of color versus color zoning—shades of lighter or darker tones that create streaks or planes of differing color.

Remember that color is the most important consideration. If the color is fine, flaws or inclusions don't detract from the stone's value as significantly as with diamonds. If the overall color or beauty is not seriously affected, the presence of flaws should not deter a purchase. But, conversely, flawless stones may bring a disproportionately higher price per carat because of their rarity, and larger sizes will also command high-er prices. In pastel-colored gems, or stones with less fine color, clarity may be more important.

*Be sure to check the stone's color in several different types of light—*a spotlight, sunlight, or fluorescent or lamplight—before making any decision. Many stones change color—some just slightly, others dramati-cally—depending on the light in which they are viewed. Be sure that the stone is a pleasing color in the type of light in which you expect to be wearing it most.

If you are considering a stone with rich, deep color—especially if it is for special occasions and likely to be worn mostly at night—be sure it doesn't turn black in evening light. Some stones, like sapphire, can look like black onyx in evening light.

Remember to give special attention to wearability. If you are con-sidering one of the more fragile stones, think about how the piece will be worn, where, and how frequently. Also, pay special attention to the setting and whether the stone is mounted in a way that will add protec-tion, or allow unnecessary, risky exposure to hazards.

Get the Facts on the Bill of Sale

If a colored stone is over one carat and is exceptionally fine and expensive, make the sale contingent on verification of the facts by a qual-ified gemologist, appraiser, or gem-testing lab such as American Gemo-logical Laboratories (AGL), the American Gem Trade Association (AGTA) Gem Testing Center, or the Gemological Institute of America (GIA).

Always make sure that any item you purchase is clearly described in the bill of sale exactly as represented to you by the salesperson or jewel-er. For colored gems, essential information also includes the following:

- The identity of the stone or stones and whether or not they are genuine or synthetic, and not in any way a composite (doublet, triplet).
- A statement that the color is natural, if it has been so represent-ed; or, in the case of sapphire, a statement that the stone is either surface diffused or *not* surface diffused.

- A statement describing the overall color (hue, tone, intensity).
- A statement describing the overall flaw picture. This is not always necessary with colored stones. In the case of a flawless or nearly flawless stone, it is wise to note the excellent clarity. In addition, note any unusual flaw that might prove useful for identification.
- A statement describing the cut or make. This is not always necessary, but it may be useful if the stone is especially well cut, or has an unusual or fancy cut.
- The carat weight of the main stone or stones, plus total weight if there is a combination of main and smaller stones.
- If the stone is to be taken on approval, make sure that the *exact* dimensions of the stone are included, as well as any other identifying characteristics. The terms and period of approval should also be clearly stated.

Other Information That Should Be Included for Jewelry

- If the piece is being represented as being made by a famous designer or house (Van Cleef and Arpels, Tiffany, Caldwell, Cartier, etc.) and the price reflects this, the name of the designer or jewelry firm should be stated on the bill of sale.
- If the piece is represented as antique (technically, an antique must be at least a hundred years old) or as a period piece from a popular, collectible period like Art Deco, Art Nouveau, or Edwardian (especially if made by a premier artisan of the period), this information should be stated on the bill of sale, with the approximate age or date of manufacture and a statement describing the condition.
- If the piece is made by hand, or custom designed, this should be indicated on the bill of sale.
- If the piece is to be taken on approval, make sure millimeter dimensions—top to bottom, as well as length, width, or diameter—are provided, as well as a full description of the piece. Also, check that a time period is indicated, such as "two days." Before you sign anything, be sure that you are signing an approval form and not a binding contract for purchase.

CHAPTER TEN

How to Select a Reputable Jeweler & Gemologist Consultant

It's very difficult to give advice on this matter, since there are so many exceptions to any rules I can suggest. Size and years in business are not always absolute indicators of the reliability of a firm. Some one-person jewelry firms are highly respected; others are not. Some well-established firms that have been in business for many years have built their trade on the highest standards of integrity and knowledge; others should have been put out of business years ago.

One point worth stressing is that for the average consumer, price alone is not a reliable indicator of the integrity or knowledge of the seller. Aside from variations in quality, which often are not readily discernible by the consumer, significant price differences can also result from differences in jewelry manufacturing processes. Many jewelry manufacturers sell mass-produced lines of good-quality jewelry to jewelers all across the country. Mass-produced items, many of which are beautiful, classic designs, are usually much less expensive than handmade, one-of-a-kind pieces, or those on which there is a limited production. The work of some designers may be available in only a few select establishments and may carry a premium because of skill, labor, reputation, and limited distribution. Handmade or one-of-a-kind pieces are always more expensive, since the initial cost of production is paid by one individual rather than shared by many, as in mass-produced pieces.

Furthermore, depending on the store, retail markups also vary based on numerous factors unique to each retailer, including differences in insurance coverage, security costs, credit risks, education and training costs, special services such as in-house design and custom jewelry production and repair, customer service policies, and more.

The best way to select wisely is by shopping around. Go to several fine jewelry firms in your area and compare the services they offer, how knowledgeable the salespeople seem, the quality of their products, and pricing for specific items. This will give you a sense of what is fair in your market area. As you do so, however, remember to ask the right questions to be sure the items are truly comparable, and pay attention to design and manufacturing differences as well. As part of this process, it may be helpful to consider these questions:

- *How long has the firm been in business?* A quick check with the Better Business Bureau may reveal whether or not there are significant consumer complaints.
- *What are the gemological credentials of the jeweler, manager, or owner?* Is there a gemologist on staff? Does the store have its own laboratory?
- *What special services are provided?* Are custom design services, rare or unusual gemstones, educational programs, Gemprint, or photographic services for your jewelry available?
- *How would you describe the store window?* Is the jewelry nicely displayed? Or is the window a mélange of incredible bargains and come-on advertising to lure you in?
- *How would you describe the overall atmosphere?* Is the sales staff's manner professional, helpful, tasteful? Or hustling, pushy, intimidating?
- *What is the store's policy regarding returns?* Full refund or only store credit? How many days? What basis for return?
- *What is the repair or replacement policy?*
- *Will the firm allow a piece to be taken "on approval"?* It won't hurt to ask. Some jewelers will. However, unless you know the jeweler personally this is not often permitted today, since too many jewelers have suffered from stolen, damaged, or switched merchandise.
- *To what extent will the firm guarantee its merchandise to be as represented?* Be careful here. Make sure you've asked the right questions, and get complete and accurate information on the bill of sale, or you may find yourself stuck because of a technicality.

If the jeweler can't or won't provide the necessary information, I recommend that you go to another store, no matter how much you've fallen in love with the piece. If you're making the purchase on a contingency basis, put the terms of the contingency on the bill of sale.

Never allow yourself to be intimidated into accepting anyone's claims. Beware of the person who says "Just trust me" or who tries to intimidate you with statements such as "Don't you trust me?" A trustworthy jeweler will not have to ask for your trust; he or she will earn it through knowledge, reliability, and a willingness to give you any information you request—in writing.

Again, in general, you will be in a stronger position to differentiate between a knowledgeable, reputable jeweler and one who isn't if you've shopped around first. Unless you are an expert, visit several firms, ask questions, examine merchandise carefully, and then you be the judge.

Using a Gemologist Consultant

Somewhat new to the gem and jewelry field is the arrival of the gemologist consultant. People interested in acquiring a natural-colored gemstone or a fine piece of period or antique jewelry that may be difficult to find in traditional jewelry stores are now seeking the professional services of experienced gemologist consultants. A gemologist consultant can provide a variety of services, including general consulting to help you determine what you really want, what it will cost, and how to best acquire it; how to dispose of jewelry you already own, or from an estate; how to design or redesign a piece of jewelry and have it made. A gemologist consultant can also provide the expertise needed to help you safely purchase gems or jewelry at auction, or from private estate sales. An experienced gemologist consultant can expand your view of the possibilities in terms of gemstones and also suggest ways to make jewelry more personal and distinctive.

As with all else in the sparkling world of gems and jewelry, be sure to check the credentials of anyone offering services as a gemologist consultant. Do they have a gemological diploma? How long have they been working in the field of gems? Do they have a laboratory? Can they provide references within the field? Can they provide client references? If you have jewelry you wish to sell, arrange meetings at a safe place, such as a bank vault.

Fees vary, depending on the gemologist consultant's level of expertise and experience and the nature of the assignment. For example, for general consulting about how to buy or sell gems or jewelry, you should expect to pay about $125 to $200 per hour for someone with good credentials.

For assistance in the acquisition or sale of specific gems or pieces of jewelry, some gemologist consultants work on a fixed fee for the project, some on a percentage of the purchase or sale amount, and some at an hourly rate. When I am retained by clients, my work is done on one of the bases noted above, or even a combination of them, depending on the nature of the work to be done and what best meets the client's needs.

If You Want to File a Complaint

If you have a complaint about a firm's practices or policies, please contact the Better Business Bureau in your city. In addition, if any jeweler has misrepresented what was sold to you, please contact the Jeweler's Vigilance Committee (JVC), 25 West 45th Street, Suite 400, New York, NY 10036, (212) 997-2002. This group can provide invaluable assistance to you, investigate your complaint, and take action against firms believed to be guilty of fraudulent activity in the jewelry industry.

CHAPTER ELEVEN

Buying on the Internet:
E-Commerce & Online Auctions

E-commerce is the current buzzword, and gem and jewelry websites are springing up almost daily, along with online auction sites. The internet offers an endless array of merchandise from around the world—a virtual international flea market—and opens doors to more choices than ever imagined, at prices often represented to be much lower than what can be found in traditional jewelry stores. Buying on the internet can be fun, and there are some good opportunities for knowledgeable buyers, possibly even a real "treasure" at a bargain price. But e-commerce and online auctions are not for everyone, and the risk of buying something that is not properly represented is very high. Before flying off into cyberspace, take a few moments to consider some of the pros and cons.

For many, the major attraction of shopping on-line is convenience. It is fast and easy, enabling you to make decisions in private, but without the assistance of salespeople. For those who live in remote areas far from fine jewelry stores, it provides an opportunity to see what is available, see what's new and exciting, and keep current about everything from gemstones to the latest award-winning designers. Many online vendors also provide educational sites to help you understand more about what you are buying. And for people who leave important gifts to the last minute, the internet can bring the world of jewelry directly to the screen, in time to be a real lifesaver!

It is easy to see the allure of internet shopping, but in all too many cases it is not all that it appears to be. Where gems and jewelry are concerned, the disadvantages may quickly outweigh the advantages, especially on auction sites.

The first disadvantage is the inability to see and compare gems and jewelry firsthand. As I hope you've learned from previous chapters, this is a serious shortcoming, since it is impossible to accurately judge beauty and desirability from a static photo. Furthermore, you can't determine how well made a piece of jewelry might be or how it might compare with the alternatives. Be sure to ask about the vendor's return policy, and read the fine print. Find out how quickly merchandise must be returned and whether you will receive a refund. Be leery of vendors who will only give a credit toward future purchases.

Another serious problem is the absence of any screening mechanism to help you determine the reliability of information provided. Sales information pertaining to gems or jewelry being sold is often incomplete and inaccurate, and many "educational" sites are also filled with inaccurate, incomplete, or misleading information. It is also difficult to find reliable information about the competence or trustworthiness of many online vendors, and written representations may be meaningless unless you can work out a way to verify the facts before making payment to the vendor.

In general, everything I have warned about in previous s applies to purchases from an online vendor or auction. As I have stressed repeatedly, many of the factors affecting quality and value cannot be accurately judged without gemological training, experience, and proper equipment, and many online vendors are so deficient in requisite knowledge and skill that their representations may be unreliable.

I cannot emphasize too strongly the importance of taking every precaution to protect yourself and ensure you are getting what you think you are getting, at an appropriate price. Remember that many internet companies and individual vendors are unknown entities, without reliable track records or well-established reputations. This means that problems might be more difficult or impossible to resolve satisfactorily, regardless of "guarantees" made before purchase. You must also remember that it may be difficult or impossible to find the seller off-line, and you cannot rely on vendor ratings because they can be easily rigged by the unscrupulous.

Appraisals and Laboratory Reports Provide a False Sense of Security

Appraisals and gem-testing laboratory reports are being used increasingly by online sellers to increase confidence among prospective buyers. Unfortunately, they are also being used increasingly by the unscrupulous. I am seeing an increase in bogus appraisals and fraudulent lab reports that have duped unsuspecting buyers into purchasing something that has been misrepresented. Be sure to get independent verification of any documentation provided by the seller before payment if possible.

Remember also that you cannot properly judge a gem on the basis of a lab report or appraisal alone. In other words, you really must see the stone along with the report.

Other problems that are surfacing on the web include the following:

- *Failure to comply with Federal Trade Commission (FTC) guidelines.* The FTC has found extensive failure to comply with FTC guidelines. Most notably, descriptions provided by sellers often omit critical information pertaining to quality factors, exact weight, and treatments used on colored gemstones.
- *Prices are often higher than fair retail.* Don't assume you will pay a lower price, and beware of fictitious "comparative retail" prices that lead you to believe you are getting a bargain. Prices are often no lower than those at a local jewelry store, and many e-retailers sell jewelry at prices significantly higher than what you would pay for comparable quality from knowledgeable, independent jewelers. Before buying on-line, check prices from a variety of sources, including your local jeweler.
- *"Wholesale" claims may be misleading.* "Wholesale" online offerings present even greater risks to consumers than buying in any wholesale jewelry district, because you do not see the actual gem or jewelry firsthand and have no guarantee you are buying from a bona fide wholesaler. Many people buying "wholesale" through online sources are not getting the bargains they believe they are getting, and many mistakes would have been avoided had the buyer seen the jewelry first or had an opportunity to compare it with alternatives.

  In some cases, arrangements can be made to allow you to view the stone before the vendor receives payment, using a local bank or gemological laboratory, for example, as an intermediary. I recommend this be done wherever possible.
- *Here today, gone tomorrow.* In numerous reported cases, buyers have never received the merchandise for which they paid, or received merchandise that was not as represented. Often there is no recourse because vendors cannot be located once the transaction is complete.

Online Auctions—Rewards and Rip-offs

Fine auction houses are an important source of exquisite jewelry from bygone eras, often exhibiting elaborate workmanship that cannot be duplicated today. They are also an important source of some of the finest, rarest, and most magnificent natural gemstones—gems that surpass even the best material being mined today—which are no longer available in the jewelry trade. Such gems may fetch handsome prices—possibly even a new record—or some knowledgeable buyer may recognize a treasure that others have missed and pay very little. This, for many, is what makes the auction arena so fascinating.

Items offered at auction may also come to the auction block to settle estates, or as a means to dispose of unclaimed property, and usually must be sold at whatever the highest bid might be, regardless of value. While this is no guarantee that you'll get a bargain, because knowledgeable buyers know the value of pieces on which they are bidding, sometimes these pieces are sold at very low prices because no one obtained proper certification and they get overlooked, even by the pros!

Buying at auction can be a rewarding experience, but keep in mind that even at the best firms there is an element of risk. One must be very knowledgeable, or work with an expert consultant, to recognize opportunities and spot pitfalls. Over the years I've seen many pieces acquired from reputable auction firms that contained synthetic stones, fracture-filled stones, and diffusion-treated sapphires!

As I have stressed throughout this book, no one can properly judge any fine gem without seeing it firsthand and examining it with proper gem-testing equipment. Where auctions are concerned, proper examination is even more critical because the auction house has limited liability. I never bid on any item at auction without having personally viewed the piece and examined it with proper gem-testing equipment. Firms such as Antiquorum, Christie's, and Sotheby's provide opportunities to view the items at exhibitions held at various locations around the country before the auction, and bidding takes place both on-site and on-line, as a convenience to people who cannot be present. However, this is not the case with all online auction sites, and in many cases there is no opportunity to view the item before bidding on it. In such cases, more than anything else, success is dependent upon having incredible luck!

Protection May Be Illusion

Where some auction sites are concerned, you may be under the impression that you are protected against misrepresentation and have recourse should there be a problem, but this may be just an illusion. In reality, you may have no recourse at all. Never forget that in situations where proper examination is not possible, the risk is dramatically increased: you are bidding on a blind item from a blind source. Even among legitimate sources, not seeing the gem or jewelry before purchase can result in disappointment when you receive your purchase. Be sure to read the "terms and conditions" very carefully, especially the fine print pertaining to "representations, warranties, and limits of liability."

Buying at auction can be an exciting and exhilarating experience with compelling financial incentives, but there are always risks for the unknowledgeable, and buying through online auction sites poses even greater risk. The FTC has warned that internet auction fraud has become a significant problem. According to the FTC, most consumer complaints center on these situations:

- Sellers who don't deliver goods
- Sellers who deliver something far less valuable than they described
- Sellers who don't deliver in a timely way
- Sellers who fail to disclose all the relevant information about the product or terms of sale

Form of Payment May Provide Protection

There are several payment options that might provide some protection. Credit cards offer the most consumer protection, usually including the right to seek a credit through the credit card issuer if the product isn't as delivered. If the seller won't agree, other options include setting up an escrow arrangement (for which there is usually a nominal fee) or using a reliable third party for verification, such as a well-known gem-testing laboratory, before an exchange of products or money.

To sum up, whether you are buying or selling gems or jewelry online—from e-retailers, auction sites, or individuals—the rewards may be great, but the risks are much higher than buying from traditional sources.

For additional information on how to reduce the risk in buying or selling on-line, or to file a complaint, write to the Federal Trade Commission, Consumer Response Center, 600 Pennsylvania Avenue, NW, Washington, DC 20580, or see their website: www.ftc.gov.

Online Sources of Information

There are many sources of online information, but there is not yet any screening mechanism to separate reliable from unreliable information. You must consider the source of the information and be wary of information provided by sellers of gems or jewelry. The following sites may provide helpful information:

1. www.ftc.gov (Federal Trade Commission)
2. www.jewelryinfo.org (Jewelry Information Center)
3. www.gia.edu (Gemological Institute of America educational site)
4. www.ags.org (American Gem Society)
5. www.gem.net (colored gemstone information site)

CHAPTER TWELVE

Caring for Your Gems & Jewelry

A key to enjoying your jewelry over the years is knowing how to care for it and protect it. I've come to realize, however, that most people don't know what proper care means. So, here are some tips that will help you derive even greater pleasure from your jewelry and gems—after you buy!

Store Jewelry Carefully

Store your jewelry carefully. Avoid *extremes* of temperature and humidity (places *very* hot or *very* cold; *very* humid or *very* dry).

Keep gemstone jewelry and gold and silver pieces separated from each other to prevent scratching. Keep fine jewelry in soft pouches or wrapped in soft cloth to help protect it.

Don't overcrowd your jewelry box. This can result in misplacing or losing pieces that might fall unnoticed from the case. Forcing jewelry into the box may cause damage, such as bending a fragile piece or cracking a fragile stone.

Handle and Wear Fine Jewelry with Care

Every twelve to eighteen months have a reliable jeweler check each fine jewelry piece to make sure the setting is secure, especially the prongs. If you ever feel (or hear) the stone moving in the setting, it's a warning that a prong or bezel needs tightening. Failure to fix this may result in loss or damage to the stone.

Get into the habit of removing jewelry before showering or bathing. Soap can deposit a film that can diminish the liveliness and beauty of your jewelry, and necessitate more frequent cleaning. Also, remove jewelry before putting on makeup or powder, and wash your hands after applying makeup (to remove dulling residues) before handling your jewelry.

Avoid wearing fine jewelry while doing any type of rough work, especially where abrasives or chemicals are used. Abrasives can scratch your jewelry—both the stones and the metal. Chemicals such as chlorine and ammonia can cause discoloration of metals used in settings and dull the polish on many stones (necessitating having the stone repolished to restore its full beauty). Chlorine (and chlorinated pool water) can cause settings to pit, discolor, and even break (especially 14K gold, or lower), causing lost stones. Ammonia will remove the polish on stones such as malachite (avoid cleaning any malachite "objets d'art" with any ammonia-based cleaner)!

Avoid exposing fine jewelry to intense heat (for example, while *cooking).* Exposure to extreme heat—from contact with a hot pot handle or from getting too near a flame or hot steam—can cause damage to many gems. *Note:* enamel may be ruined by contact with heat. I know someone who ruined an antique ring with lovely enameling on the shank by picking up a pot with a very hot handle that caused the enamel to melt.

Avoid storing jewelry in safe deposit boxes for extended periods of time. While rubies, sapphires, and diamonds won't be adversely affected, other gems—such as opal and emerald—may suffer from the extreme dryness. With these gems, if long-term storage in a safe deposit box or bank vault is unavoidable, place a damp cloth in the box with the jewelry (check from time to time to be sure the cloth is still damp).

Avoid exposing fine jewelry to extreme temperature changes, such as might be encountered by putting jewelry in an in-the-ground safe in winter or in an automobile trunk while traveling, then removing it and wearing in a heated room. This is especially important with opals.

Never boil jewelry to clean it. Stones may crack or lose their color.

Special Tips on Opals and Emeralds

Immerse opals in water for a few minutes periodically to help prevent loss of moisture and subsequent cracking. *Never immerse opals in oil;* soaking some opals in oil for only a few hours can cause them to lose some or nearly all of their fire. *Note:* it was once thought that wiping the surface of an opal regularly with oil would protect it. *This is not true and will damage most opals.*

Avoid wearing emeralds while doing rough work or active sports. Emeralds are fragile and are susceptible to damage from a hard blow or a knock.

Never clean opals or emeralds in ultrasonic cleaners. Ultrasonic cleaners can worsen inclusions and weaken color.

A Few Special Words about Rings

Try not to touch the stones in your rings when putting them on or taking them off. Instead, take rings on and off by grasping the metal portion that encircles the finger (called the shank). Slipping rings on and off by grasping the metal shank rather than the stones will prevent a greasy buildup on the stone's surface, which greatly reduces the brilliance and sparkle of a stone.

To keep rings sparkling, get into the habit of "huffing" them. This is a little trick we use to remove the dirt and oily film on the stone's surface (which occurs from putting rings on and off incorrectly, or from occasionally fingering them—which most of us do without even realizing). Each time the stones are touched, a layer of oily film is applied to the top, and the stone's beauty is reduced. To restore its sparkle, simply hold the ring close to your mouth and "huff" on it with your breath—you'll see the stone fog up—and wipe it off with a soft, lint-free cloth, such as a handkerchief, scarf, or coat/blouse sleeve. You'll be amazed to see how much better jewelry can look simply by removing even the lightest film of oil from the surface!

Don't take rings off and lay them on the side of the sink unless you are sure the drain is closed. Also, never remove your rings to wash your hands when away from home (all-too-many have been forgotten and lost).

Take Extra Precautions When Traveling

If you take jewelry with you when traveling, don't pack it in luggage that you plan to check or in luggage to be given to the bell captain at a hotel or a ship's porters, etc. Keep it with you.

Never leave jewelry in your hotel room. Wherever possible, obtain a safety deposit box in which to store your jewelry, even for part of a day. Be wary of in-room safes that are operated by programming your own private code; professionals can quickly and easily override your code and remove the contents of the safe.

Purchase a "body pouch" that can be concealed under clothing for when you *must* carry a valuable piece. Never go sightseeing with valuables in a purse or pocket.

For customs purposes, it can be useful to take a photo (a simple Polaroid) of the jewelry pieces you take with you. Have the photo dated and notarized before departure, so you can prove that you did not purchase it abroad. Otherwise you may be asked to pay duty on it.

Keep a Photo Inventory of your jewelry. You don't need professional photos; simply lay your jewelry out on a flat surface and take several snapshots. They will be invaluable should there be a robbery, providing detectives with a visual record that will make it easier to recognize the stolen pieces and claim what is yours should the jewelry ever be recovered. Photos are also important for insurance purposes and can aid in replacement. Where a piece is one-of-a-kind, and you want to have someone make a replica, a photo can provide a custom jeweler with the necessary details in order to duplicate it.

Keep Your Jewelry Clean to Make It Sparkle

Keeping your gemstone jewelry clean is essential if you want it to sparkle to its fullest. Film from lotions, powders, and your own skin oils will dull stones and reduce their brilliance. You will be amazed at how much a slight film can affect the brilliance—and color—of your gems. So, learn how to keep them clean, and clean them on a regular basis.

How to Clean Your Jewelry

The simplest and easiest way to clean any kind of jewelry is simply to wash it with warm sudsy water. Prepare a small bowl of warm sudsy water, using any kind of *mild* liquid detergent. Soak the piece a few minutes and then brush gently with an eyebrow brush or soft toothbrush, keeping the piece submerged in the sudsy water. Rinse thoroughly under running water (make sure the drain is closed—some prefer to place jewelry in a wire strainer before placing under the running water) and pat dry with a soft lint-free cloth or paper towel.

Ruby and sapphire jewelry, especially pieces containing diamonds, can be immersed in a solution of equal parts of hot water (not boiling— you should be able to put your fingers in it without pain!) and ammonia. This can be especially effective at removing built-up dirt and grime. Let the jewelry soak for a few minutes, brush gently, rinse well, and pat dry with a lint-free cloth. Remember, however, that ammonia should *not* be used on most other gems, and washing with warm, sudsy water is usually sufficient for *all* gemstones.

Use Jewelry Cleaners and Ultrasonic Cleaners with Caution

Commercial jewelry cleaners usually are no more effective than the methods suggested above. They seem to be popular because they are convenient. In any case, *never soak gemstone jewelry in commercial cleaners for more than a few minutes.* Leaving stones such as emerald or amethyst in some commercial cleaners for any length of time can cause etching of the surface, which reduces the stone's luster (shine). For difficult pieces, try the new *ionic* cleaners. These are safe for all gems—even emeralds and opals—and are fast, convenient, and affordable.

I do not recommend ultrasonic cleaning for most gems—the new ionic cleaners are safer and equally effective. Ultrasonic cleaning should be restricted to the cleaning of diamonds or gold jewelry only. Washing in sudsy water or using an ionic cleaner is simple, effective, and safe for all jewelry.

A Selected List of Recognized Laboratories

American Gemological
  Laboratory (AGL)
580 Fifth Avenue, Suite 706
New York, NY 10036

American Gem Trade Association
  (AGTA) Gemological Testing Center
18 East 48th St., Suite 1002
New York, NY 10017

CISGEM-External Service for
  Precious Stones
Via Ansperto, 5
20123 Milano
Italy

European Gemological
  Laboratory (EGL)
30 W. 47th St., Suite 205
New York, NY 10036

Gemmological Association and Gem
  Testing Laboratory of Great Britain
27 Greville St.
London EC1N 8SU
England

Gemological Association of All Japan
Katsumi Bldg., 5F, 5-25-8
Ueno, Taito-ku
Tokyo 110
Japan

Gem Certification and Appraisal Lab
580 Fifth Avenue, Suite 1205
New York, NY 10036

Gemological Institute of America
  (GIA) Gem Trade Laboratory (GTL)
580 Fifth Avenue
New York, NY 10036

Gemological Institute of America
  (GIA) Gem Trade Laboratory (GTL)
5345 Armada Dr.
Carlsbad, CA 92008

Gübelin Gemmological Lab
Maihofstrasse 102
CH-6006 Lucerne 9
Switzerland

Hoge Raad voor Diamant (HRD)
Hoveniersstraat, 22
B-2018 Antwerp
Belgium

International Gemmological Institute
579 Fifth Avenue
New York, NY 10017

Professional Gem Sciences (PGS)

5 South Wabash, Suite 1905
Chicago, IL 60603

550 South Hill St., Suite 1595
Los Angeles, CA 90013

Schweizerische Stiftung für Edelstein-
  Forschung (SSEF)
(Swiss Foundation for the Research
  of Gemstones)
Falknerstrasse 9
CH-4001 Basel
Switzerland

Selected Readings

Arem, Joel E. *Color Encyclopedia of Gemstones.* New York: Van Nostrand Reinhold, 1987. Excellent color photography makes this book interesting for anyone. An invaluable reference for the gemologist.

Downing, Paul B. *Opal Identification and Value.* Tallahassee, Fla.: Majestic Press, 1992. For the serious opal lover. Retail price guides.

Gübelin, Eduard, and J.L. Koivula. *Photoatlas of Inclusions in Gemstones.* Zurich: ABC Editions, 1986. Most comprehensive collection of inclusions ever photographed.

Keverne, Roger, ed. *Jade.* New York: Lorenz Books, 1996. Superb, encyclopedic; 450 lavish photos.

Matlins, Antoinette L. *Engagement & Wedding Rings: The Definitive Buying Guide for People in Love.* 2nd ed. Woodstock, Vt.: GemStone Press, 1999. Beautiful photos of rings from fifteenth century to present.

Matlins, Antoinette L., and A.C. Bonanno. *Gem Identification Made Easy: A Hands-On Guide to More Confident Buying & Selling.* 2nd ed. Woodstock, Vt.: GemStone Press, 1997. A nontechnical book that makes gem identification possible for anyone—even without a science background. A "must" for beginners, and the experienced may pick up a few tips, too. Practical, easy to understand.

Nassau, Kurt. *Gemstone Enhancement: History, Science, and State of the Art.* Woburn, Mass.: Butterworth's, 1994. Comprehensive and understandable.

Schumann, W. *Gemstones of the World.* Translated by E. Stern. New York: Sterling Publishing Co., 1977. Superior color plates.

Sinkankas, John. *Emerald and Other Beryls.* Tucson, Ariz.: Geoscience Press/Harbinger House, 1982. A classic work on the beryl family.

Zeitner, June C. *Gem and Lapidary Materials: For Cutters, Collectors, and Jewelers.* Tucson: Geoscience Press, 1996. A beautifully illustrated book about gemstones and how they are fashioned into works of art.

Color Plates and Exhibits

Black-and-White Photographs and Illustrations

All illustrations by Kathleen Robinson.

Page 34: Cabochon emerald ring by Jack Abraham, President of Precious Gem Resources.

Color Photographs

We wish to thank the following persons and companies for the color photographs appearing in this book:

Page 1: Courtesy of Jack Abraham, President of Precious Gem Resources.

Page 2: Star ruby from International Colored Gemstone Association (ICA) (photo/Bart Curran). Selection of red and pink gemstones and rhodochrosites from Pala International, Inc. (photo/Sky Hall). Red beryl from Rex Harris (photo/Sky Hall).

Page 3: Star sapphire and moonstones from International Colored Gemstone Association (ICA) (photos/Bart Curran). Selection of blue gemstones from Pala International, Inc. (photo/Sky Hall). Chrysocolla from American Gem Trade Association (AGTA), cut by Glenn Lehrer, AGTA Cutting Edge competition winner (photo/Sky Hall). Blue Paraiba tourmaline from Cynthia Renee Co. (photo/Robert Weldon).

Page 4: Selection of yellow and orange gemstones from Pala International, Inc. (photo/Sky Hall). Topaz from American Gem Trade Association (AGTA) (photo/ Natural Arts, Inc.). Sunstone from Ponderosa Mine, Inc. (photo/Bart Curran). Sapphire, andalusite, and cat's-eye chrysoberyl from Krementz Gemstones (photo/Sky Hall). Fancy-cut citrine with concave facets from American Gem Trade Association (AGTA), cut by Cutting Edge winner Richard Homer, American Lapidary Artists (photo/Sky Hall). Yellow beryl from AGTA, cut by Cutting Edge winner Karl Egan Wilde (photos/Sky Hall).

Page 5: Selection of green gemstones and tsavorite garnet from Pala International, Inc. (photos/Sky Hall). Emerald-cut emerald from International Colored Gemstone Association (ICA) (photo/Sky Hall). Paraiba tourmaline from Cynthia Renee Co. (photo/Robert Weldon). Laboratory-grown synthetic stones from Chatham Created Gemstones. Period Art Deco jadeite brooch from Christie's, NY.

Page 6: Andamooka crystal opal, Andamooka matrix opal beads, and two free-form black opals from Western Opal (photos/Sky Hall). Mexican opals and oval cabochon black opal from International Colored Gemstone Association (ICA) (photos/Bart Curran).

Page 7: Briolettes from Rough and Ready Gems (photos/Azad). Trilliant from David Brackna (photo/Robert Weldon). Oval, round, cushion, and emerald cut from John Parrish Photography. Marquise and pear shape photos by Sky Hall. Princess from Lucent Diamonds™ (photo/Tino Hammid). Cabochons from James Alger (photo/Van Pelt).

Page 8–13: All courtesy of the gemstone cutters, artists, designers, and companies listed. (Michael Christy/Susan Allen photos by Michael Christy; Virginia Anderson and Karen Feldman photos from Geoffrey Kudlick for Jewelers of America.)

Page 14: Emerald cuts, clockwise from top left, from: Antiquorum Auctioneers; Barnett Robinson; Russ Copping, from Geoffrey Kudlick for Jewelers of America; James Breski; and Barnett Robinson. Princess cuts from Chris Correia. Henry Dunay's rings from Henry Dunay. Brian Sholdt's ring from Brian Sholdt (photo/Aaron Cheney).

Page 15: Top row from James Breski. Middle row, from left to right, from: a private collection (photo/Tibor Ardai); Barnett Robinson; and Precious Stones Company. Bottom row from James Breski.

Page 16: Belt buckles from Elizabeth Rand Studio. Stone cabochons and beads photo by Sky Hall.

Index

178

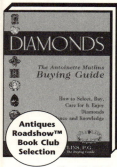

DIAMONDS: THE ANTOINETTE MATLINS BUYING GUIDE

How to Select, Buy, Care for & Enjoy Diamonds with Confidence and Knowledge

by Antoinette Matlins, P.G.

Practical, comprehensive, and easy to understand, this book includes price guides for old and new cuts and for fancy-color, treated, and synthetic diamonds. **Explains in detail** how to read diamond grading reports and offers important advice for after buying a diamond. **The "unofficial bible" for all diamond buyers who want to get the most for their money.**

6" x 9", 220 pp., 12 full-color pages & many b/w illustrations and photos; index
Quality Paperback Original, ISBN 0-943763-32-0 **$16.95**

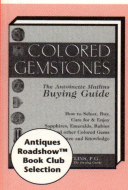

COLORED GEMSTONES:
THE ANTOINETTE MATLINS BUYING GUIDE

How to Select, Buy, Care for & Enjoy Sapphires, Emeralds, Rubies and Other Colored Gems with Confidence and Knowledge

by Antoinette Matlins, P.G.

This practical, comprehensive, easy-to-understand guide **provides in depth** all the information you need to buy colored gems with confidence. Includes price guides for popular gems, opals, and synthetic stones. Provides examples of gemstone grading reports and offers important advice for after buying a gemstone. **Shows anyone shopping for colored gemstones how to get the most for their money.**

6" x 9", 224 pp., 16 full-color pages & many b/w illustrations and photos; index
Quality Paperback Original, ISBN 0-943763-33-9 **$16.95**

THE PEARL BOOK: THE DEFINITIVE BUYING GUIDE, 2ND EDITION

How to Select, Buy, Care for & Enjoy Pearls

by Antoinette Matlins, P.G.

COMPREHENSIVE • EASY TO READ • PRACTICAL

This comprehensive, authoritative guide tells readers everything they need to know about pearls to fully understand and appreciate them, and avoid any unexpected—and costly—disappointments, now and in future generations.

- A journey into the rich history and romance surrounding pearls.
- The five factors that determine pearl value & judging pearl quality.
- What to look for, what to look out for: How to spot fakes. Treatments.
- Differences between natural, cultured and imitation pearls, and ways to separate them.
- Comparisons of all types of pearls, in every size and color, from every pearl-producing country.

6" x 9", 232 pp., 16 full-color pages & over 250 color and b/w illustrations and photos; index
Quality Paperback, ISBN 0-943763-28-2 **$19.95**

The "Unofficial Bible" for the Gem & Jewelry Buyer

Antiques Roadshow™ Book Club Selection

JEWELRY & GEMS:
THE BUYING GUIDE, 5TH EDITION

How to Buy Diamonds, Pearls, Colored Gemstones, Gold & Jewelry with Confidence and Knowledge
by Antoinette Matlins, P.G., *and* A. C. Bonanno, F.G.A., P.G., A.S.A.
—*over 250,000 copies in print*—

Learn the tricks of the trade from *insiders:* How to buy diamonds, pearls, precious and other popular colored gems with confidence and knowledge. More than just a buying guide . . . discover what's available and what choices you have, what determines quality as well as cost, what questions to ask before you buy and what to get in writing. Easy to read and understand. Excellent for staff training.

6" x 9", 320 pp., 16 full-color pages & over 200 color and b/w illustrations and photos; index
Quality Paperback, ISBN 0-943763-31-2 **$18.95**
Hardcover, ISBN 0-943763-30-4 **$24.95**

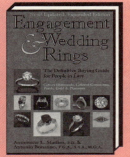

• COMPREHENSIVE • EASY TO READ • PRACTICAL •

ENGAGEMENT & WEDDING RINGS, 2ND EDITION
by Antoinette Matlins, P.G., *and* A. C. Bonanno, F.G.A., A.S.A., M.G.A.

Tells **everything you need to know to design, select, buy and enjoy that "perfect" ring** and to truly experience the wonder and excitement that should be part of it.

Updated, expanded, filled with valuable information.

Engagement & Wedding Rings, 2nd Edition will help you make the *right* choice. You will discover romantic traditions behind engagement and wedding rings, how to select the right style and design for *you*, tricks to get what you want on a budget, ways to add new life to an "heirloom," what to do to protect yourself against fraud, and much more.

Dazzling 16-page color section of rings showing antique to contemporary designs.
Over 400 illustrations and photographs. Index.
6" x 9", 304 pp., Quality Paperback, ISBN 0-943763-20-7 **$16.95**

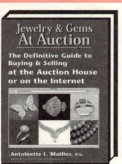

JEWELRY & GEMS AT AUCTION
The Definitive Guide to Buying & Selling at the Auction House or on the Internet
by Antoinette Matlins, P.G.

As buying and selling at auctions—both traditional auction houses and "virtual" Internet auctions—moves into the mainstream, **consumers need to know how to "play the game."** There are treasures to be had and money to be saved and made, but buying and selling at auction offers unique risks as well as unique opportunities. This book makes available—for the first time—detailed information on how to buy and sell jewelry and gems at auction without making costly mistakes.

6" x 9", 208 pp. (est.), fully illustrated
Quality Paperback Original, ISBN 0-943763-29-0 **$19.95** (Avail. February 2002)

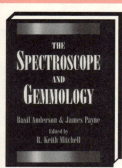

Buy Your *"Tools of the Trade..."*

Gem Identification Instruments directly from *GemStone Press*

Whatever instrument you need, GemStone Press can help.
Use our convenient order form, or contact us directly for assistance.

ITEM / QUANTITY	PRICE EA.*	TOTAL $
Lamps—Ultraviolet & High Intensity		
_____ Small LW/SW (UVP)	$69.00	_____
_____ Large LW/SW (UVP)	$189.00	_____
_____ Viewing Cabinet for Large Lamp (UVP)	$147.00	_____
_____ **Purchase Large Lamp & Cabinet together for $299 and save $37.00**	$299.00	_____
_____ High Intensity Lamp (Eickhorst)	$600.00	_____
_____ Dialite Flip Lamp (Eickhorst)	$64.95	_____
Maglite		
_____ Large Maglite	$15.00	_____
Refractometers		
_____ Standard Refractometer (Eickhorst)	$625.00	_____
_____ Pocket Refractometer (Eickhorst)	$495.00	_____
_____ Refractive Index Liquid—10 gram	$42.50	_____
Spectroscopes		
_____ Spectroscope—Pocket-sized model (OPL)	$89.00	_____
_____ Spectroscope—Desk model w/stand (OPL)	$225.00	_____

Shipping/Insurance per order in the U.S.: $4.95 first item,   SHIPPING/INS. $_____
$3.00 each add'l item; $7.95 total for pocket instrument set.

Outside the U.S.: Please specify *insured* shipping method you prefer and
provide a credit card number for payment.   **TOTAL $** _____ **

Check enclosed for $ _____ (Payable to: GEMSTONE PRESS)
Charge my credit card: ❏ Visa ❏ MasterCard
Name on Card _____
Cardholder Address: Street _____
City/State/Zip _____
Credit Card # _____ Exp. Date _____
Signature _____ Phone (_____)_____
Please send to: ❏ Same as Above ❏ Address Below
Name _____
Street _____
City/State/Zip _____ Phone (_____)_____

Phone, mail, fax, or e-mail orders to:
GEMSTONE PRESS, P.O. Box 237, Woodstock, VT 05091
Tel: (802) 457-4000 • *Fax:* (802) 457-4004 • *Credit Card Orders:* (800) 962-4544
www.gemstonepress.com
Generous Discounts on Quantity Orders

See Over for More Instruments

TOTAL SATISFACTION GUARANTEE
If for any reason you're not completely delighted
with your purchase, return it in resellable condition
within 30 days for a full refund.

*Prices, manufacturing specifications, and terms subject to change
without notice. Orders accepted subject to availability.

**All orders must be prepaid by credit card, money order or check
in U.S. funds drawn on a U.S. bank.

017

Cut along dotted line

...LINS BUYING GUIDE   5/02
_____ copies s/h*

DIAMONDS: THE ANTOINETTE MATLINS BUYING GUIDE
_____ copies at $16.95 (Quality Paperback) *plus s/h**

ENGAGEMENT & WEDDING RINGS: THE DEFINITIVE BUYING GUIDE
_____ copies at $16.95 (Quality Paperback) *plus s/h**

GEM IDENTIFICATION MADE EASY, 2ND EDITION:
A HANDS-ON GUIDE TO MORE CONFIDENT BUYING & SELLING
_____ copies at $34.95 (Hardcover) *plus s/h**

GEMS & JEWELRY APPRAISING, 2ND EDITION
_____ copies

ILLUSTRATED G
_____ copie

JEWELRY & GEM SELLING
AT THE AUCTIO
_____ copie

JEWELRY & GEM
_____ copie
_____ copie

THE PEARL BOO
_____ copies

THE SPECTROSC
_____ copies

TREASURE HUNT
WHERE & HOW RALS—
IN 4 REGIONAL VO
_____ copies of NE S   copies of SW States

* In U.S.: Shipping/Handli
Outside U.S.: Specify sh

- -

Check enclosed for
Charge my credit c
Name on Card (PRIN
Cardholder Addres
City/State/Zip _____
Credit Card # _____ Date _____
Signature _____)_____
Please send to: ❏ S
Name (PRINT) _____
Street _____
City/State/Zip _____)_____

TOTAL
SATISFACTION
GUARANTEE
If for any reason you're
not completely delight
ed with your purchase
return it in resellable
condition within 30
days for a full refund.

Prices subject
to change

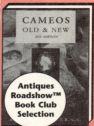
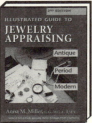
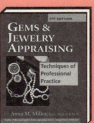